A Voice in the Silence of Noise

A Voice in the Silence of Noise

To Live Sovereignly in a Non-Sovereign World

By, A Gardener Who Walked Away

A Voice in the Silence of Noise

First Edition
ISBN: 978-1-0678387-2-0
Catalog No. SP-03

Published by: Sovereign Phenomenology Press.
Printed in Canada

To the remembering, the return, and the truth that we are never lost.

What we call being lost is only the moment before remembering.

Also by A Gardener Who Walked Away,

Garden Victory: The Day I walked away from the rented war.
The Table View: The Mechanics of the Rented War.
A Voice in the Silence of Noise: To Live Sovereignly in a Non-Sovereign World

Chapter 1: The Internal Territory.

Silence. It is quite the word; to listen to nothing. Just the quietness within, to not hear the constant chatter around us. Or the constant voice in our heads. The silence of just hearing the ambient sounds around us drown into the sounds of nothing. Where even our own heartbeats fade into a quiet resonance of nothing, really.

For myself, I live in a world now where the silence is in abundance. The noise of the outrage matrix and rented wars is just a fading memory—slowly and gradually fading into the silence and nothing that has taken the place of the deafening noise. Some may say it is just a void that has to be filled by something or anything. A void that must be occupied to pass the ever-marching steps of time.

For myself these days, I have come to find that the "void" of silence and nothing is not really a void at all. To me, it feels like a nurturing place in which to heal—not only mentally, but physically and spiritually as well.

An internal place inside of me that is just as vibrant as the gardens of life outside. I have come to understand that the silence within and without is a place where our entities truly thrive.

A place that is at odds with the external polar opposite of the outrage matrix itself. As now I see the outrage matrix as the true void in this world—where it sucks the energy out of us, creating an endless cyclone of constant conflict. That is the true void, a place that we inadvertently end up in, and one that becomes almost impossible to escape. A true void, or a place of hell, a person could say. If they look a step farther, yet—hell itself is a human creation.

So is there really a true hell? Or just a place we like to call it? It is tough to say. Some people enjoy living in their human-made hell, while others try desperately in vain to escape it. But as I said, hell is a human creation—a creation meant to keep us in fear. Just as the rented wars intend us to be.

The whole concept for me would be the outrage matrix that thrives and feeds off our negative emotions and outrage, just like the digital world wants. Personally, I do understand that it all goes a lot deeper than that. However, I will just leave that thought for now.

As much as I have an abundance of silence and "nothing," for lack of better terms, people do not have enough silence and "nothing." People express that thought all the time—that the only thing they wish for is a moment of peace. Away from the hectic and busy lives they have created for themselves. To sit in the mornings and watch the sun rise with a cup of tea or coffee.

To sit in the present moment and feel the silence—a way to start the waking day on a good note. To know that our time sovereignty means something.

I am sure we have all been in the same boat at some point in our lives, if not all our lives. The whole ideal of time sovereignty, in which we feel compelled to spend every waking moment on this planet doing something. Jamming as many activities as possible into the day to "feel" like we are living in the moment, yet never actually taking time to listen to the silence of our inner beings. To shut off the noise and our egos, to just listen to our hearts beat and the sound of a ticking clock moving time forward.

As for when we do take the moment, do we not feel like we are always interrupted? By the sound of a phone, or a young family member asking to be entertained because they are bored. Or just the voice inside saying that laying or sitting in silence is a waste of time, as we should always be doing something. Anything.

It is truly incredible how we trained ourselves from birth to ignore the one thing that truly matters the most in life—the silence of nothing in our minds and the world around us. We really did do it to ourselves by subscribing to the rented wars of others. We kind of do only have ourselves to blame. For whatever reason, we thought it best to remove ourselves from the silence.

To become forever entrapped in the noise of the matrix. At this point, we are just born into it. It has become our lives in so many different ways. Whether it be enlisting our children into every program, sports team, or educational camp we can think of to make sure they will succeed, to all the academic programs possible.

Whereas our older selves look back upon the past, scrolling through the Rolodex of our memories, we see how every last waking moment was filled with others' rented wars. With no real chance to find ourselves in the silence that was given to us. I do not see this as some sort of blame game on my part; I am just telling it as I see it. Where, as we get older, we see our own pasts missed as others lived vicariously through us—just as we live vicariously through the youth around us.
At that point, are we actually free sovereign entities? Or just trapped once again in an endless loop that the outrage matrix and rented wars entrapped us in?

This year is different, though. This year I continue on my journey of digital abstinence—a complete unsubscribe from social media. So this morning, I am sitting with a coffee next to me, typing my thoughts away, listening to the ferocity of Mother Nature's power while I prepare myself for another day at the office. One thing that I have found is that the silence of the world sure helps me prepare mentally for the day. No checking social media for updates, no watching the morning news for current events. Maybe just checking the weather to see how the day will be. With, of course, some time to write down my thoughts of the morning.

Honestly, my decision to leave social media has nothing to do with a New Year's resolution or the fact that I felt trapped or anything like that. The main reason I left it all was because I just found it boring.

That is about it. I saw it all as an endless loop of conflict in which the conflicts never get resolved—they just mutate into a different conflict. Same ideas, just different skins. It became nothing new, just something demanding my attention that I felt was best spent elsewhere.

I do understand that my perspective differs from many others in this world in terms of social media. Some would now call me a hermit; others could say that I took back my individual sovereignty from the grasp of the collective consciousness the internet created. As well, I do understand that many people these days are looking for a way to disconnect—to become one with the silence. In the lives we have manufactured for ourselves, through the constant need to always be busy. To once again fill our waking moments with "activity," not leaving any downtime for our minds and bodies to relax and feel safe. We have been taught and told that silence and boredom are our enemies in this world—that they are not condoned. An ideal that is a threat to the machine itself, as in quietness, the outrage matrix cannot touch us.

The irony of it all is that we have been warned numerous times about the outrage matrix. Not only have been warned, but are constantly being warned about the machine that steals our time for its profits.

Unfortunately, as much as we are being warned about the machine, the vast majority ignore the warnings because the message comes from the most unlikely sources. Sources that the machine itself views as a threat, ultimately labeling them as evil or noise.

That is a bit of a cruel one. The machine sees the warnings and truth of itself as noise to be blocked, yet the machine drowns out our silence with noise to block the silence.

It always seems to be whatever makes the loudest noise to block our silence that wins.

I saw it all as an endless loop of conflict in which the conflicts never get resolved—they just mutate into a different conflict. Same ideas, just different skins. It became nothing new, just something demanding my attention that I felt was best spent elsewhere.

I do understand that my perspective differs from many others in this world in terms of social media. Some would now call me a hermit; others could say that I took back my individual sovereignty from the grasp of the collective consciousness the internet created. As well, I do understand that many people these days are looking for a way to disconnect—to become one with the silence. In the lives we have manufactured for ourselves, through the constant need to always be busy. To once again fill our waking moments with "activity," not leaving any downtime for our minds and bodies to relax and feel safe. We have been taught and told that silence and boredom are our enemies in this world—that they are not condoned. An ideal that is a threat to the machine itself, as in quietness, the outrage matrix cannot touch us.

The irony of it all is that we have been warned numerous times about the outrage matrix. Not only have been warned, but are constantly being warned about the machine that steals our time for its profits. Unfortunately, as much as we are being warned about the machine, the vast majority ignore the warnings because the message comes from the most unlikely sources. Sources that the machine itself views as a threat, ultimately labeling them as evil or noise.

That is a bit of a cruel one. The machine sees the warnings and truth of itself as noise to be blocked, yet the machine drowns out our silence with noise to block the silence. It always seems to be whatever makes the loudest noise to block our silence that wins.

Chapter 2: Attention As Territory.

Growing up, I had always marched to a different drumbeat in life. I never really looked for popularity or acceptance from the circles of people in my younger years. I decided to keep more to myself for the most part. I was never after being the life of the party, nor did I look to be the center of attention. I preferred to just be "there."

Of course, I had numerous friends from numerous places. It seemed that I enjoyed individual relationships over collective ones. I would become friends with one person from a larger group, form a bond, enjoy our time together, and then, when it was time, move on to the next person. Most of my individual friendships did not end in malice or hate. They usually just faded away, leaving on a positive note of mutual respect, as all of us still ran in the same groups.

Just as much as I had individual friendships with males, I had the same with females—many of them. Not in a relationship sort of way, but in platonic friendships where the hormones were put aside so we could bond through mutual respect and understanding. There was never any hanky-panky involved, and none of us saw anything wrong with it.

But my female friends and I knew one thing: it created resentment among the males in the circles I lived in. They viewed me as a threat, mostly because they were the ones with crushes on the girls I was close with. It's comical now that I think of it. The males would confide their crushes to me, and the females would do the same. And in the end, no one ever had a crush on the person who had a crush on them. It was always someone else.

But I digress. At the end of it all, it just felt more natural to have individual friendships within the youthful tribes that were created, rather than trying to be the leader of the tribe. I came to understand at a young age that friendships are not meant to last forever. They are meant to last for as long as the present moment requires. I guess the best way to put it is, "We are not here for a long time, just a short time."

Within the bigger tribe of friends I had landed in, there were always smaller tribes within. We were all just a loose group, broken down into smaller groups. Nothing really set each smaller tribe apart from another; the only thing that did was our tastes in music. Although we were all like-minded people who shared the same common interests and ideologies, music was the only decisive issue.

In one corner, there was the group that only listened to pop music—Britney Spears, New Kids on the Block, Maroon 5, and the like. In another corner, the strictly country group. On the other side, the heavy-metal group: AC/DC, Pantera, Metallica. And then there was the rap and gangster group, which was quite the sight to see— a bunch of teenagers raised in a blue-collar, conservative background, rapping to the likes of Snoop Dogg, Dr. Dre, and the NWO. It was an eclectic mix of people at gatherings, yet no one really argued or fought. Music differences aside, we all knew we were in the same boat in life..

Well, except for me. I found a different beat altogether—one that most people found rather distasteful, for lack of a better word. My go-to music was a mixture of classical pieces such as Beethoven, thanks to my father's cassette tapes he left in the car. As I waited for him while he visited work acquaintances, curiosity and boredom usually got to me. I would randomly pick cassettes and listen to them, which opened my musical world to the likes of Jethro Tull, Deep Purple, and of course, Led Zeppelin. Music I genuinely enjoyed listening to, far more than what my peers gravitated toward. Eventually, my musical tastes evolved into my own, and the industrial genre lured me toward bands such as Nine Inch Nails, KMFDM, My Life with the Thrill Kill Kult, and of course, Tool.

I can never forget Tool or Maynard James Keenan. Maynard —now there is one guy who got shafted by the matrix. People always wondered why there was such a long pause between Tool albums. That was certainly the work of the matrix and the record studios, if I remember correctly.

To me, the music of the other smaller tribes around me never really appealed. I didn't mind the heavy-metal groups, but a person can only take so much of the screaming of Pantera or the long droning of Ozzy Osbourne. Country music was simple enough: "My truck broke down, and my dog died. My wife left me, so I am going to drown my sorrows in a bottle of whiskey." Rap and gangster music never appealed either—listening to people talk or sing about smoking blunts, "cappin'" someone, and pouring low-grade beer on the ground. Each to their own, I suppose.

As for pop music, that is just bubble-gum music. Which is exactly that—music meant and designed for radio stations, and that's about it. All the Britney Spears, Madonnas, boy bands, and girl bands. It is all the same: artificial, synthesized music created to be perfect, with not one key out of tune.

I learned that concept from my older brother, who was a music engineer in a larger city in our younger years. I ended up at his place, and he took me to work at the studios. The first night, it was just a small band who partook in some marijuana and then sat there jamming through endless riffs, letting the music drift from their souls. The next day, it was another band. They had all the equipment and gear, where they would play for a while and then sit there digitally retuning the music—note by note—as if they were superstars. I found it rather boring. As we left, my brother told me that was "bubble-gum music"—music that is not going anywhere; they just think it will.

The concept stuck with me. Now I could hear the artificial or commercial tones in other music.

It does seem like all music is designed that way—the bubble-gum way—for commercialization of the product. Not for the words or rhythms that flow naturally, the raw emotional aspect of music. Some may say that my style of music is just that—commercial noise of the matrix, such as Nine Inch Nails —which one could say is technically true. However, with Trent Reznor, the noise is the machine. The long, grinding mechanical riffs of the songs are the nature of the machine—the sounds and noises masked behind the bubble-gum music thrown at us.

In retrospect, music really is in the eye of the beholder. We use the whole idea of music to fill the gaps in our days. Instead of listening to the monotonous drone of long travels in our vehicles, we switch on the radio to remove the silence, to give ourselves a distraction or noise to listen to. In the same breath, as we go about our daily chores at home, we put on music to kill the silence around us—noise to fill the atmosphere, to distract from the mundane tasks that life presents us. Or we use the noise of music to simply tune out the world around us, just as we do at the gym or when taking public transportation. Music has turned into a crutch that we use to escape the silence that rests on the edges of our worlds.

I picked Nine Inch Nails as an extreme example of those who show us the machine called the outrage matrix. Over the years, I ended up finding other music in the oddest of places that also captures the tones of the outrage matrix and rented wars. Most hide in obscure spots, lost in the machine—yet never lost to time, as the internet is truly forever. Usually, the message hides in the fast-paced music and lyrics of the industrial genres, with bands such as KMFDM. Their flag song, "A Drug Against War," is a high-powered, fast-paced track with a theme exactly like the title: a drug against war. Our apathy toward the rented wars is what stops the rented wars. It is the same concept as unsubscribing from someone else's wars—

not through civil disobedience, but through the apathetic approach of being stoic, or as I called it, “passionately indifferent.”

Chapter 3: Pacification Arm.

Today, I elected to make this day a lazy Saturday. A day to just be a couch potato and listen to music; not to drown out the silence of the day, but to complement the silence. The silence that now is deeply rooted in my mind from leaving the noises of social media — the outrage matrix and the rented war that almost all subscribe to. I think today is January 17, 2026. As I look to a calendar — why yes. Yes, it is the 17th of the first month of the year. I suppose I should feel proud of myself. In another four days, it will be a full two months since walking out of the gates.

This lazy Saturday, the music of choice is A Perfect Circle — long, drawn-out melodies and the deep, haunting voice of Maynard James Keenan. Music intended to draw us inward through melancholy, through the drifting harmonies and subtle rhythmic tensions. Followed through with the deep undertones of the voices that sing away, almost creating a sense of suspended tension meant to catch us in a moment where we just exist alongside the music itself. Music that ebbs and flows like the tides of the ocean, drifting us in and out of our perceived realities. Not through yelling or dominating, but by just quietly whispering to us.

It is certainly a different type of music that emanates from Maynard James Keenan. His lyrics flow with the intricacies of the rhythm and melodies of the playing instruments, creating a story in our minds — a story that encourages a person to escape within ourselves. To see the world through our internal lenses; to know that there is more to the world beyond the external noise that lies around us. Almost like a well-tuned orchestra that has been weaponized against the outrage matrix itself, lying in its own arm of the main branches of our concept of music. Off in a place the outrage matrix despises; in an architectural lineage all of its own. I suppose a clearer term would be the "Sovereign Lineage." The category of music that does not subscribe to the outrage matrix, nor subscribe to the rented war. In fact, it can be viewed as the counter to the machine. Music that is created independently from the machine. Music that does not pick a side in the tribal warfare that runs rampant across the earth. Nor does it try to pacify us into a state of conformity. Nor does the music run on our emotions to elicit a reaction from us. It is music that is just there, to draw us inward into ourselves. To live freely in the moment, unsubscribed.

Just like other bands over the decades, Maynard James Keenan lands his concept of music in the heart of the sovereign lineage many others have landed in over the decades. Different, uncaring to the critics. Caring to the people who listen to the music. Unbreakable against a system that thrives on breaking the will and spirit of many.

I guess when I take the time to ponder the concept of music, it seems that the 1960s were the real kick to the variations in the music we see today. A person can indeed go farther back in time to map the progression of how music evolved from hitting sticks on stones and strumming on the intestines of a freshly killed and gutted animal. Or Grug gently serenading Ourg through a series of melodic grunts and groans. Although, a person could theorize that primitive music from humanity's early childhood could be seen as the true root of the modern-day sovereign lineage of music, as that primitive music came truly from the heart and soul — just cave people making the earliest form of noise and music to complement the silence. Pure, truthful music before music was poisoned by the outrage matrix. A time before it became known that music can be used to manipulate people to fight rented wars by drawing on their emotions — to have people react, subconsciously or consciously.

Once again, just as the economic and politically skinned rented wars of the outrage matrix, the 1960s were the pivotal moment for humanity, as well as for music. This is once again when our wonderful friend called the television made its debut in homes in every place it could find. It was the television and the new concept of mass media that grew the different limbs of the direction of music. As much as we would like to think that the counter-war protests and human rights movements were the main causes of the branching of music, it was the deeper mechanics of the outrage matrix that pushed forward the branches. Not only was it the normalization of the television in homes, but it was also the advancement in mass media such as the production of records and the utilization of the radio. Now the machine had a way to spread its version of music to millions of people instantaneously. It was truly a pivotal time in our musical history. Not only was there a way to broadcast music; it could now be used by the corporations and governments to relay a message to us — through the use of emotionally charged songs to mobilize or pacify us. Even going to the extent of catering to different groups and ideologies. Even going as far as creating new genres that target the youth of our societies, just like the economic skin of the rented war, our children were now viewed as a commodity by the machine. Our well-being has never mattered to the outrage matrix — just our subscription and our tithes. That is all it is after; that is all it cares about.

To talk about pacifying: back in the 1960s, there was a big anti-war movement happening as people were finally tired of the endless loops of rented wars. With that came the anti-war music movement — songs and themes designed to take a stance and not follow the "Man" into battle, to die for someone else's cause. These were accompanied by anti-war protests and sit-downs. Yet now that we know the machine uses music to pacify us, how do we know that the anti-war songs were not just the machine quelling the noise by using artists to its advantage? Whereas the anti-war music was a way to stop the anti-war movements by just making people feel better that something was being done about it — through the word of song?

At this point, some may argue that the machine created the anti-war music movement as a false representation. Which I can see; on my part, it is more of an over generalization of the concept, which leads to the true splintering of the musical tree. Whereas the artists that produced the music created the new branch of the tree through creating the "activation arm." Whilst in their haste to get their message out, they relied on the same system that carries out the rented wars — the corporations — who in turn took the message of the music and diluted it by tempering and dulling the message. So much that it became "sedated." In which the true message of rallying the troops against the rented wars became a message — a feel-good message that, through emotions, made people react subconsciously that the outrage matrix cared about them.

Here we stand, at the pivotal point in human history. Where on one side we have music that activates us. On the other side, we have music that sedates us. In the forgotten middle, we have the forgotten music — the music of the source code; the sovereign lineage. At this point, I do have to acknowledge that I am not demonizing, nor am I promoting one particular group over the other. I am just merely pointing out how the outrage matrix and rented war engineered music to either pacify us or activate us. Really, the mechanisms are opposites in reality, though. They are the same — just different sides of the coin.

The concept of bubble-gum music is a well-known one. It is attributed to the brand of music that tends to be on the side that aims at pacifying the listener through an idealized form of escapism. The whole concept really hit mass media back in the 1960s with bands such as The Beach Boys, The Monkees, as well as The Archies. These three bands were the prime architects that led to the evolution of the sedation branch. These three bands stand out in particular in a time of social unrest and never-ending wars. People were looking for escape from the noise, in which The Beach Boys certainly delivered a product in which to escape. Through their music, they created a whole mythical world of California — singing about cars, surfing, and the free life of living carefree.

People would be swept away by the music as if they lived on the beaches themselves. A world where the other skins of the outrage matrix could not touch them.

Through the mythology of California that The Beach Boys created, people did flock to California, believing that they could truly escape. Yet, as many people migrated west to the sunny beaches of California, they were struck with the real-world realization that California was the same as any other place in the world — the same fragmentation of society, the same high costs of living, even fewer jobs. The disappointment of the realization that it was the same machine, just a different skin. In the end, the band was not actually promoting California. They were providing people with the concept of escapism, which proved impossible for most people. In a sense, they created an ideal that was impossible to achieve, yet most people bought into it.

It was not the only band to use such an ideal to pacify the audience into a false state of belief. Over the years, other noticeable bands would use the same architecture as The Beach Boys. Another notable band would be the 1980s band Wham!. At that time in Britain, the socioeconomic situation was in dire straits due to the economic policies of the time — mainly with high unemployment rates that left many in financial dire straits. In which the band Wham! was the British version of The Beach Boys. Through its music, Wham! offered the same escapist ideals, with songs about tanning, hitting the beaches, dancing in the cabanas — essentially living life on a tropical paradise where the concerns of the real world were left far behind. Yet in all the escapism, does a person truly escape? Or just switch the chains that bind us to another anchor on the wall?

As always, the tentacles of the matrix are not just content with involving themselves in one aspect of life. It prefers to touch every aspect of our worlds. Just as with the creation of the band called The Monkees — a band that was not really a band per se. It was a band of actors who relied on childish and clownish antics to appeal to the younger generations. Our youth. Whereas the band members were not actual musicians, but actors. The whole concept was to provide a contrast to the other genres of the time — the drug-fueled hippy genres. In which the band's main goal was to provide people with a sense of innocence, where the band used its antics as more of a sanitized rebellion, one that a child could identify with, as well as let parents be comfortable with the acts of the show. In a sense, they had learned how to manufacture innocence by providing a more sanitized version of the current events. Obviously, this led to the future genre of groups that acted like bands, yet were just actors — all directed at children to provide a more "child-friendly" experience while still maintaining the undertows of society.

As we move forward past the concepts of idealistic escapism and manufactured innocence, the sedation arm of our now engineered music continues to grow. Of course, the engineering is never complete if our favorite chemical — dopamine — is not added into the mixture. Which now it is, although it is almost tragic that dopamine is always right at the center stage of the outrage matrix. It truly is the chemical that keeps the machine running. Just as in the next band: The Archies, where the whole concept of "bubble-gum pop" or "bubble-gum music" stems from.

Bubble-gum music, in essence, is usually just one-hit-wonder groups that once again target our youth to invoke dopamine loops in the listener through basic melodies and catchy phrases repeated over and over. The music itself is basic in its complexities. Whereas by keeping it simple, it is engineered for the ears of our children. Catchy words and phrases are used to constantly spike our dopamine levels in a constant loop. I'm sure we all have heard similar songs throughout our lives — catchy songs that have very simple lyrics that repeat, where the music itself lacks any sort of depth behind it. Yet it keeps us engaged, or the song gets stuck in our heads. Just like the song "Sugar, Sugar" by The Archies.

At this point, it becomes rather clear as to why they used the word "sugar" in a children's song — as it was designed for just that reason: to spike dopamine levels, as within our own biology sugar is a natural dopamine spike when we ingest it. In the mechanics of the bubble-gum system, that is what they rely on — words that keep us engaged by tapping into the chemistry of our minds. Once the bubble-gum mechanics were established, using the dopamine-loop concept never faded away. The concept changed skins to match the audience of the decades to come, just as the band NSYNC and the singer Ariana Grande had capitalized on. If you were to listen to their music, you can hear the same mechanics that the earlier bubble-gum concept had used.

At this point, the architecture of the sedation arm had really started to grow into new ways, as the corporate machine looked for other ways to pull in the masses. Whereas the musical engineers developed new ways to emotionally pull people in. At this point in the mechanics, the music industry had swayed away from the organic structure of what music is really about toward the manufactured, corporate mechanics that persist to this day — a process in which the music is on an assembly line of musicians, singers, instruments, digitizers, synthesizers; all designed to create music that does nothing but sell.

In all honesty, for myself, this is the part where I see music lose its true heart and soul — the organic human component — to be replaced with the digital version. Whereas the true form of the music is torn to shreds, thrown in a blender, and remixed just for the profits. That is where bands such as ABBA come to light. As with ABBA, I am sure we have all heard songs from them over the years. The band ended up taking the sedation arm to a whole new level. As history shows, ABBA was big into the synthesization of their music during production, in which they would meticulously cut apart their music to piece it all back together for the masses. Using techniques that layered the different instruments upon each other, ultimately creating a "wall of sound," according to the experts, with layering in the voices to create a chorus effect for the listener — ultimately creating an engineered euphoria of music.

By creating an engineered euphoric atmosphere for the audience, ABBA created an environment of brainwave entrainment, where the performance overrode the brain's chemistry to allow high releases of dopamine. Some say it could have a person reach levels similar to those on ecstasy. This time around, the dopamine levels were not the only target of the engineered music, but the levels of cortisol in a person as well. Using mathematical formulas, ABBA trained their music to run along the same principles as neural beat frequencies. It did create a collective trance-like setting for the people who frequented such shows.

Just as with the other engineered music of the sedation arm, the concept was adopted into modern-day pop music. We just don't know about it. Yet now we do. It is crazy to think at this point that music truly was engineered to pacify us in ways we would not even know about. But shall we continue on? At this point, I do believe that the mechanics are emerging that the machine has indeed engineered the music we listen to in ways that give a reaction without us even knowing. In a sense, as these bands strive for "musical" perfection, they are creating an analog system that can hack our brainwaves, in which our brains give out a chemical response. After a short breath, I am almost led to believe that these musicians were not really musicians at all. The way they figured out how to hack into our minds and brainwaves — I would almost have to say that they are neurosurgeons or psychologists with the way they engineered their music. Especially with the likes of the Bee Gees, The Carpenters, and later on, the likes of Ed Sheeran.

As with ABBA, the Bee Gees and The Carpenters relied on a similar mechanic in terms of their production of music. Through the production techniques both bands used, they relied just as heavily on the voices of the singers to create their own euphoric atmospheres for the listeners. Although the techniques were relatively the same, the pitches were opposite. The Bee Gees relied on higher-octave vocals in synchronicity with each other. The Carpenters relied on the single deep voice of the singer. Giving two different results, yet fulfilling the same goal — to immerse the listener in a deep sense of passiveness, relying on the sound waves to unlock chemical responses in our minds.

Although the ideal is the same, the concepts are quite different. For the Bee Gees, they relied on emotional smoothing as the mechanism behind their music, in which they employed the use of sad and melancholy lyrics with high-energy rhythms that created an atmosphere where the listener could experience heartbreak and pain through the upbeat physical joy of dancing. Thus "smoothing" the pain while keeping people happy and dancing. It is almost like an oxymoron — sing about pain and misery, yet dance and party like there is no tomorrow.

The concept did turn out exceptionally well for the Bee Gees, as the result was that the music created neurochemical reactions in the body. Not as much dopamine this time, but more along the lines of an oxytocin release in the body, which created a sort of emotional ecstasy for the listener.

Just as the Bee Gees relied on the higher pitches, The Carpenters relied on the lower pitches to achieve the same results — a result that led to soft emotional pacification. By using the same concepts as ABBA but in a lower, intimate pitch, it gave the listener a feeling of intimacy with the singer, which led to a comforting wall of sound, in which it sounded like the vocal was sitting next to the listener hand-in-hand, letting the listener sit through the pain of the song. The effects were the same — it created the same neurochemical responses as the music of the Bee Gees: a trigger of oxytocin with a sense of calmness and safety. At this point, we all have to ask ourselves: for those who listened to such music over the years, did we actually like the music? Or was it all just an engineered fabrication of reality? Whereas our minds were hacked by the analog algorithms that were meticulously created. When we listen to such music, are we truly listening to it of our own sovereign will? Or are we just being held prisoner by the frequencies of the music that affect our brain chemistry?

The sedation arm does not stop there — it simply evolves into a new tentacle that ensnares us. Just as the boy bands of the 1990s and on. I am sure we have all heard of the pioneering band Backstreet Boys. This particular band was pioneering in a way most would not have seen at the time. It was not in the sense of the concept of the bands; it was the concept behind the engineering of the band.

From the beginning, just as the assembly-line manufactured bands that were created in the past, the same concept was used with New Kids on the Block. In a sense, the band was carefully crafted and put together using the "average person" from the working class to give the illusion that they were "one of us." By having them viewed by the audience as being one of the "gang," so to speak — by acting like they were just everyday people. Through their music, they conveyed the idea that they were just everyday people, giving the listener the feeling that they were one of them. A part of the gang, in which the listener would develop bonds with the singers of the bands. Creating a sense of friendship which the band preyed upon. The more outgoing and inclusive to the audience, the greater the parasocial dependency created — the audience all feels like they are "in" with the group, yet the group does not even know the listener is there. I am sure we have all seen this parasocial dependency in avid fans of such bands. They do come to a point where they truly believe they are a part of the band. However, in all honesty, the band itself was engineered in such a way.

In a sense, the group Backstreet Boys performed in a similar way as the engineered parasocial techniques of NKOTB, just in a different form — emotional outsourcing. As much as the words of their songs lacked depth and substance, they parroted people's emotions so much that it drew people in emotionally. Creating an atmosphere where the empty words that were sung by no one but many band members gave the feeling of safety in numbers to the listener. Whereas it created a situation of "emotional outsourcing" for the listener — a concept where the band really doesn't sing about anything important. It uses just enough words and rhythm to draw in the listener, where the listener surrenders emotional control to the song. Almost like our modern-day algorithms of the outrage matrix, which in all honesty is one and the same — using emotionally charged analog music to have us surrender our emotions, to be caught up in the rented war of another. All the while, our emotions are harvested by the outrage matrix. It is all the same mechanics — just different skins and variations. As we approach the end of the sedation arm for now — as in the future, there will be one more that comes along before the ultimate switch to tailor-made artificial intelligence music, where AI will be the final frontier of the sedation arm. A frontier where the digital algorithms use our emotions to create music specifically for our emotions in the moment. We reach the final architect.

Through the combinations of all the engineered concepts — the engineered euphoria of ABBA, the smoothing effects of the Bee Gees, the relatability and parasocial dependency created by the other bands — Taylor Swift took all of the proven concepts and rolled them all up to create the final structure of the sedation arm. By combining all the previously engineered architecture, she created the ultimate fusion: "parasocial emotional outsourcing." This particular concept has proven to be quite potent, looking at her success using such a concept. By tapping into the inner emotions of her audience, as well as using the mathematical framework of the previous bands, she created an environment through engagement to let her fans feel like she understands them all, by providing real-life emotional experiences to them. Through the music, she provided the same sound effects as the previous bands in terms of reaching a certain neurological effect through our brain chemistry — all orchestrated to create a mass following that sees her as a "cultural system" to many.

Ultimately putting her in a position where people don't listen to her music — they live inside her music. Through using frequencies of her music to tap into our dopamine release, as well as convincing people that they can relate to her, she has created another prison of the outrage matrix. In which the rented war that others fight on her behalf is all an engineered product on Taylor Swift's part, to ultimately harvest people's emotions for her wealth — all the while entrapping people inside the outrage matrix.

Chapter 4 Activation Arm.

A new day, a new chapter in life. I sit once again as I have done for the last 60 days of my life. The window curtains open, a warm morning coffee in hand, waiting for the sun to peek over the horizon, basking the world in beautiful shades of pink and reds, waking the slumbering world around. As I sit here in the morning silence I have come to embrace, only disturbed by the slow ticking of the clock on the wall, I ponder the last two months of my life. When I made my escape from the digital world, I did not know what to expect. I honestly thought that I would have fallen back into it by now; remarkably, I have not.

I have certainly left that world behind me. No more beeps or pings of devices going off at random times, nor is my time spent endlessly chasing digital rabbits throughout the day. Nor is my time spent arguing against ideas in the digital coliseum. I actually feel at peace with myself; I feel alive in such a different way that it is almost hard to explain.

I have noticed the changes in my life. At first, they were just subtle changes, such as feeling like time has slowed down; the days do not feel rushed anymore. My mornings and evenings move at just the right pace — my pace. I don't feel rushed anymore from hours of doom-scrolling or checking apps for the latest events whenever I can. I feel free now that I have reclaimed my time sovereignty. To me, that is the biggest part of life we should all cherish. Just as much as we should cherish our families, cherishing our time is just as important.

In my time outside of the outrage matrix, I have noticed a lot of positive changes within. My anxiety has disappeared, where I feel balanced within myself now. I don't have any thoughts of negativity — I just feel peaceful inside. A feeling that I had not felt in the longest time. Just feeling content in life. I have also seen a drastic change in my own personal demeanor, as nothing bothers me anymore. Just living in the present, moving forward by the ticking of the clock. Not moving forward from one digital event to the other. I find it's an extremely blissful state to be in. Although there is one rather interesting, unseen consequence that happened. I have noticed that my sense of smell has become more acute. Along the way, I noticed that smells became stronger; I didn't think much of it. Until I did a little research into it; apparently, as our minds restructure themselves away from the modes of constant fight-or-flight, we enter a different mode of safety, in which our minds slow down and our senses become more acute. We become further connected to one of the true source codes located internally within ourselves.

As with all, the day must get on. Back to the cycle of "working" to pay for life. Back to living in a little bit of the matrix as I enter the building to the constant noise of the local radio station playing in the background. More music, more noise. With that, another walk back into the outrage matrix to explore the mechanics of the machine — to view and see the wiring and schematics of the machine that seeks to control every aspect of our lives. I do continue to listen to music — or the noise, I should say. As I arrive at work, the noise is always playing in the background — an old ghetto blaster from an era gone by faithfully plays the music of old on the local radio station. Just background music to liven the atmosphere of the workplace.

Where I am at, there are only two radio channels to pick from: country or rock. As country becomes rather depressing after a while, rock it is — or I should say 1970s to 1990s music, which is a little ironic. All things considered — perhaps that is why I am inclined to shine a light on these subjects.

Depending on the day, the frequencies of the music change. As of today, it is good old "rebel" music meant to get us in an upbeat tempo with the classic rock of KISS, The Who, with a splash of Nirvana and the Rolling Stones. These days, no one ever thinks of the classic rock songs of the past as "rebel" music — more like just relics of the past. From a different era in time, yet at the inception of the songs played, they were considered revolutionary and rebellious music. Almost all of the rock bands dating all the way back to the 1960s are songs of rebellion in one way, shape, or form. Just as the concept of the "activation arm," the music was engineered to "activate" us or have us led to believe that we are or were a part of a rebellion against the "man," as they used to say.

Yet was the music truly engineered for true rebellion? Or was it engineered in a way that led us to believe in the illusion that we are rebelling?

That seems to be the premise of the rock genre — to give the illusion of being free and rebellious in a fight against the man. The concept took off with the creation of the Rolling Stones with their edgy style and looks. They engineered their style of distorted frequencies; they created a style of noise that stimulates a fight-or-flight response within the mind. Whereas a listener could feel like they are a street fighter, ready to take on anything or any war — yet all the time, the listener just sat in their bedroom with the rock tunes blazing.

The Rolling Stones were essentially the grandfather architects of the musical modern-day rented war, as by creating an environment of "street fighting," for lack of better terms, people would be empowered and buy into the Rolling Stones' concept for fighting as per their music. It was not the only theme that they put forth. They were all about sex, drugs, and rock 'n' roll, in which the whole rebel concept became a purchasable product. A listener can act and feel that they are rebels for a cause, yet they are still purchasing the concept by buying into the Rolling Stones. By starting with the Rolling Stones, who are the grandfathers of the modern outrage matrix engineered toward us through their music, they show us that sex, drugs, and rock 'n' roll — or outrage — is more profitable than pleasure. In terms of rebelling itself, they created an atmosphere of managed rebellion, whereas everyone plays the act of rebelling, yet no one actually rebels.

Just as The Who. They were masterclass at the illusion of rebelling, although their engineered performances differed from the Rolling Stones. As much as the Rolling Stones were about sex, drugs, and rock 'n' roll, the theme behind The Who was creating division between the young and the old by creating an assault on the establishment. By using themes that it is you vs. them — young vs. old — or the whole ideal that a person would rather die before becoming old. It established a generational firewall in society, whereas youth do not see a future for themselves, as "live free and die hard" was the better way to go. (I am sure at some point in our youth we have all thought that: I am 18 now. There is no point in planning a future as I will be dead by then.) It is rather morbid thinking, yet that is what the music told us. In terms of engineering a you-vs-them, they engineered a you-vs-ourselves, as when we get older, we have nothing to offer the world; it is only when we are younger that we prove any worth to the world. It truly is the work of the outrage matrix and the rented war — subscribing to an ideal that tells us that we should not live old enough to see the sovereign lineage.

It doesn't end for The Who, as we shine the light on the outrage matrix. As much as the Rolling Stones were the "heel" in the mechanics, The Who were the industrialized agents. As with all, they did engineer their own mechanics on the assault of our minds. Just as ABBA and the Bee Gees, The Who created their own acoustic weaponry to assault us. It was in the form of the "power chord." Just a simple chord but with massive sound, designed to bypass our thoughts and hit our adrenal glands — to spike the level of adrenaline in our systems. I am sure many have been to concerts of any genre where there are towers of amplifiers and speakers to create a wall of noise, just as the ones of the sedation arm produced a wall of noise. It's the same concept, just simplified — a loud blast of noise at the right frequency that vibrates into a listener. Almost like an acoustic weapon of sorts. The results?

I am sure we can all see and say that the concept of blasting us with high-intensity vibrations worked, as people live in that music today. I am sure, though, the people that blare the bass and such from their vehicles probably have no idea what those vibrations and frequencies are doing to their brainwaves and bodies.

It does seem that is what it is all about — a concept through the use of engineered music in which musical frequencies are used against us. Although it is not only just the frequencies; it is the themes and words of the music as well. Just as in the case of The Doors and Jefferson Airplane. Their models are similar in nature, as they create an escapist world for the listener.

On one hand, you have The Doors that use more of a "shamanic" performance to capture the ear of the listener. On the other hand, you have Jefferson Airplane, who uses "a frequency of disorientation" on the listener.

Looking at The Doors first. I am sure many have listened to the prophetic singing and almost shaman-like themes that came from The Doors. In a sense, what they were engineering was the concept of a Dionysian figure — just as the lizard king persona that Jim had created. In which, by following the band, a person would be led "to the other side" or to personal salvation. It was a great concept at the time, however quite misleading. Just like the prior band, The Who, the great misconception lies with the ideal that we should die early, breaking our own mechanical lineage of our own future. Or as in some songs, it was best to stand in the house fire we created ourselves — a theme that ultimately leads to the self-destructive path of oneself. It is strange to think that the outrage matrix prefers us to stay young, but then again, growing old and wise to the world, we come to a point where we can see the machine for what it is — a mechanism that does everything to keep us from our sovereign selves.

Just as with Jefferson Airplane — another band that promoted rebellion through the spiritual skin of enlightenment. There is one song that does stand out: the song about a white rabbit, in which the song starts slow, building a hypnotic rhythm and state for the listener. Almost like a psychedelic ride of transition. That is a song that I have listened to quite a few times, back in the times of my own escapism. What better song than one about Alice taking different concoctions all the while chasing the rabbit. I never really thought about it until the time I was immersed in the grey skin of the outrage matrix. Whereas the "white rabbit" takes on a central role as everyone goes down rabbit holes in search of the truth. Which struck me as odd, as with Alice — all she does is chase the rabbit, ultimately ending back up at the surface. Or in a different context, people go down the rabbit holes to never surface again. To me, it is like the concept of "chasing the dragon," in which a person addicted to drugs is always chasing a better high. Instead of drugs, people are chasing the rabbit in search of the truth — which is always just out of reach, and the deeper they go, ultimately ending up in their own prisons.

As much as these two bands were selling the idea of transcendence, all they were actually doing was selling a different product of the matrix. As we all know, Jefferson Airplane did transform into another group, showing that the true idea of rebellion could just be re branded into another form. Just as The Doors showed they could sell a pseudo-sovereign ritual that captured the spirit of a generation, ultimately turning the whole concept into a dead-end myth. With Jefferson Airplane showing that any band can become a part of the media by being a spokesperson for a generation.

Yet, through all of it, they both showed that there was no way out — just one exit door leading all the way back to the same coliseum that a person just left. Through singing about rabbits, telling people to drop out of life, even to one particular song that is at "the end," which tells us to kill the father, they were effectively severing the link from our sovereign elders — our older selves. In reality, they turned the "great awakening" into a "great collapse." As once again, the music was engineered to cut the tie between being young and growing old. If anything, these bands showed the outrage matrix that a rebellion can be branded. Whereas all a person had to do was wear beads as a form of protest, all the while "living in the moment" with no regard for the future. As we all die young anyway. So far, through all the free-loving music and acts of rebellion — even the acts of destroying instruments at the end of a show, which magically reappeared for the next show — it proved the foundation of the modern outrage matrix. For as long as the noise was turned up so high it vibrated through a body, with spectacles of destruction, as well as layering messages within, all the while being paid by the very machine they all say they fight against.

So far, they have shown that a rebellion can be re branded, as well as showing that rebellion can be profitable to the outrage matrix. Just as the Sex Pistols of the 1970s, which were a hybrid engineered combination of The Doors, The Who, and partly of the Rolling Stones. Whereas the Sex Pistols' slogan was "no future," just as the previous bands sang about — severing the sovereign lineage of a new generation.

The mechanics of the Sex Pistols were quite the same. What is the point of changing something that works? Although by shining a light on the Sex Pistols, the mechanics become rather obvious. The Sex Pistols did not start as some sort of garage band as most would expect. They had actually started in a boutique called "Sex." It does show that the rebellion that the Sex Pistols were all about was pre-styled. As they adorned their pins and torn clothes and the attitude they wrapped up into one package, they used the same engineered music of multi-tracked guitar walls as well as the shouting and screaming in their music. It created dissonant entrainment within the listener that kept the listener in a loop of reactive agitation — just bouncing around in place while not actually going anywhere.

Looking back at the mechanics so far, the whole effect of these bands was to trap the youth in the permanent present of the outrage matrix. In a context that we were to subscribe to their rented war — a rented war with the ideal that we have no future or the world is ending. So spend our last "rent" money on the soundtrack to the collapse. Ironically, they sold us the concept that old age is not worth it, that the world would collapse, so there is no sense in planting the seeds of our own garden for the future. All the while telling us to chase the white rabbit and follow the lizard king to the other side. All the while, the very same people that told us this profited from the very matrix they were against. In all honesty, it can all be called the "Rock 'n' Roll swindle." Just as the Sex Pistols proved in glaring light — if you scream "anarchy!" loud and long enough, the fact can be hidden that the band is signed to a major global conglomerate. Where the real swindle is not money within itself.

It is stealing the activation energy, or the energy of our youth, and grinding it all down into a nihilistic dead end.

A person can disagree with my last statement, but is that not what they did? Engineer music that could tap into the primal high-octane energy of our youth, effectively tapping and grinding that energy down until the youth became empty vessels? All the time the bands were allied with the very machine they fought against? Some may view the outrage matrix and rented war as a modern digital concept. Yet it is a very old idea. In terms of the activation arm as of now, these concepts do show the analog version of our modern-day matrix. I can go one step further to say that the concepts were pioneered for the evolution from the analog to digital outrage matrix. All of the schematics and mechanics are there, exposed by the light — or hidden behind masks.

I never thought about how significant masks are to our culture in terms of what they represent. It was not until the great pandemic of the 2020s that I realized how significant masks really are. During that time, the populace was told that we must wear masks to protect ourselves from a deadly virus. It made sense — take the utmost precautions to protect ourselves. Many embraced the idea, while many outright refused the idea. Myself? I just did what I had to do to be left alone. It wasn't until I started to notice other patterns in life that showed there might be more to masks than protection from a virus.

The most obvious, of course, is to conceal one's identity, just as the ones involved in political unrest or the ones that commit crimes. The one pattern I did not notice is the concept of wearing a mask for the purpose of creating de-individualism within a tribe in an effort to subjugate the people into a hive-mind identity. Just as the band Slipknot has demonstrated. As the idea is mainly taken from the band KISS. Slipknot took the concept to a whole new level. As much as KISS used the concept of masks and makeup to become avatars, which allowed the fans to project their entire identity onto the character, Slipknot used numbered masks as a way of removing the humanization from the equation — to act as a mechanized unit. With the hive-mind attitude that came from the de-individualization of the audience, it helped convince the listeners that sovereign identity was a burden, with the answers only being found in surrendering their name and face to the hive. Although the tribal mechanics were relatively the same, the two bands differed in many ways, as KISS was the prototype, with Slipknot being an evolutionary step.

As with KISS, they showed the "total eclipse of art by spectacle" by industrializing the concept of the identity tribe — and they did it very well. By removing the "friction" of the human personality through their masked avatars, they engineered the ideal of digital euphoria before the digital age. Through their engineered music, they created a spectacle for the audience. If you have ever been to a KISS concert, you would see exactly that — a spectacle of fireworks and other pyrotechnics used to activate our primitive minds, promoting a fight-or-flight response once again. It really was not about the music itself; it was all about the show, as well as creating a product in which people could identify with. As much as they sold a show, their main push was through the concept of the KISS militia, by utilizing themes and military terms to create, once again, an us-vs-them theme. Where once again, through the use of the concept of the identity tribe, they led people to believe that they were a part of the KISS army — you lived, wore, and swore to KISS. In which now, the music, as emotionally hollow as it is, is just a delivery system for the product: everything KISS. KISS credit cards, toys, coffins — you name it. It was all about the name of the product, by convincing people that they must have the product to be a part of KISS.

At the end of it all, KISS did prove one thing: that people will pay to be sedated with a spectacle and be loyal to a brand, as long as they have a cool uniform and are led to think that they have sovereignty over their own personal identity.

But alas, home is where the heart is, is it not? Just as the sweet home of Alabama. With some of these bands, it is quite obvious — the engineered mechanics behind their music. Yet with some bands, it is not as obvious. Just as with the regional identity created by Lynyrd Skynyrd through the defensive entrainment engineered for their hit song "Sweet Home Alabama." A song we all are familiar with. In all honesty, the song was created mainly as a counterstrike to Neil Young's "Southern Man," effectively creating a binary conflict between the "outsider" and "the local." As you can see, it is another division tactic just as the others. By engineering the song into a lineage anchor, through the anthem frequencies of a triple-guitar lead layered into three distinct lines, they created a sound that felt physically unmovable — giving the listener the feeling of an unchanging landscape in their minds. Through the use of defensive entrainment, they gave the people of the South a song that defended their ancestral home's honour.

By engineering music that led the listener to believe that they were defending the honour of their lands, Lynyrd Skynyrd opened the door to the whole concept of targeted tribalism in the music world.

As much as some bands use the concept of de-individualism by cloaking themselves in anonymity to create tribalism within their audiences, others continued the evolution by pushing the limits of engineered tribalism — just as in the case of the band Guns N' Roses, in which they acted as the tribal glue of it all. In this part, by engineering hyper-reactive masculinity, GNR created a philosophy that through destruction, chaos, and addiction, they showed the listener that being rebellious meant being a self-destructive consumer. Where the listener felt like they were breaking the law by just listening to the music, yet all they were doing was following a pre-packaged script rebellion right to the record store.

As much as Guns N' Roses focused on hyper-reactive masculinity, Mötley Crüe perfected the engineered concept of chaos as a controlled environment. Whereas they sold chaos as a product, combining chaos and the high-tech circus — just as KISS and their pyrotechnics — all the same primal activations to keep the mind in a state of alert. Even with the music itself, it created a narrative for disaster. Through the concepts of sex, drugs, and rock 'n' roll; even through the band's own personal stories of arrests, overdoses, and crashes. As they documented themselves, they used the fuel from these actions to give the band street cred. For lack of better terms once again, they showed that sovereignty was found in self-destruction.

As much as Guns N' Roses and Mötley Crüe claimed to dislike each other, they were from the same coin — perhaps at most, opposite sides of the coin. Just as much as Axl Rose's raspy, high-pitched voice acted like a biological alarm to the mind — an alarm triggered by frequencies of human distress and predatory alerts that emanated from Axl's voice

— Mötley Crüe created a surgical sound that was loud and aggressive, yet the frequency was tamed for maximum volume.

From the primal screams and maximum volume, the machine can switch frequencies to match any of those that listen. Such as the tritone frequencies of Black Sabbath — or the flattened fifth of the Devil's interval, as some call it. Or we can say: "the spiritual hazard zone" that Black Sabbath engineered. Through the use of down tuning, they engineered a frequency of slow, crushing tempos that mimic our deep sleep — almost like a trance-like effect on the mind, whereas the frequencies and music itself created a superstitious danger response.

Just as the low tempos, Black Sabbath was more of a controlled opposition for the religious and political establishments. That was established through the darker themes of life, as they drew heavily on the occult and the satanic themes of the world. Which did help create the modern taboos of today within certain skins of the outrage matrix. Whereas the use of crosses and doom and gloom created a bipolar feedback loop. While the industry sold demonic rebellion to the youth through Black Sabbath, the establishment could sell moral safety to the parents. Which really shows that now "Satan" has become a product to sell — all the while, the real evil was people's souls being captured in a binary fight where they cannot see that the gate is open.

As you can see by now, whether it was all intentional or not, the activation arm created an environment of entrapment of the people through engineered music. From the beginning with the birth of the rebel product of managed rebellion, moving through the spiritual deception of the rebellion myth, to the tribal identities that lead in numerous ways, we end up at one more room before we leave this sector of the machine. (Which is fine by me. I cannot hear the noise of the machine, as the silence from within acts as earplugs to the noise. Yet I can sense the matrix and its rumbling frequencies. When that point starts moving in, it is time to go back to the garden.)

So shall we continue this guided tour, to shine the light on the last room? As shown by a few other bands in terms of de-individualization, two other notable groups took the concept to another level, combining the concepts of masked spectacle of KISS and the spiritual dread of Black Sabbath. These two band engineers used the latter bands to create a concept of total aesthetic interface, or polarization as a product. Whereas the group Ghost has engineered an institutional cycle of "killing" their old leader and "installing" a new one — essentially copying the same idea as the succession of kings and popes, creating a simulated lineage. To the point, the listener feels a sense of ancestral history with the band itself. In their music, they do use a polarized concept of satanic/pop music, creating a moral-friction neutralization, so to speak. In a better term, it would be like listening to ABBA sing about the occult and satanic themes. As with the formation of the digital age, this group has embraced the technology as well. By creating virtual-reality cathedral experiences, they have moved the machine from playing a show to operating a religion. Just as the next band, Sleep Token — a band that further engineered the concept of a digital religion born from the mechanics of their music.

As with previous groups, Sleep Token uses the same engineered tactics of anonymity of masks, with the music being filled with the same theta-wave suggestibility as a religious ritual. Once again, the themes are heavily reliant on the occult, alchemical symbols, offerings, and of course, a deity mythology built in that the group "offers" to. Just as much as Ghost can be seen as a simulated clergy, Sleep Token can be seen as the "algorithmic cult." In which the same concept as Ghost has been employed — using a virtual-reality room, "The Room Below," as their own "virtual-reality cathedral," creating a sense of total immersion for the person.

At this point, I can make a pretty good comparison to the grey skin of the matrix. Sleep Token does utilize the concept of "sunk-cost sovereignty" quite well, in terms of creating a product that has people decoding the mythologies that they put out. In which the labour of thousands of hours of decoding binds the person so tightly, they become a prisoner to the machine. As they have invested too much time of their "self" to leave — creating a state where a person would vigorously argue their case rather than admit they were chasing a manufactured sovereignty.

By employing such a concept, the two bands really did create a concept where it is not about selling songs anymore — it is selling the deity. Where worship becomes a digital utility activated on demand. A utility that both bands have captured: Ghost with the engineered concept of neural incentive, where the fans receive digital blessings based on their bio metric participation; Sleep Token with their bio metric ritual where the heartbeats of the audience are synchronized to the drum patterns of the drummer. This brings man and machine together in the final stages of somatic capture. The audience is no longer a community — it is a synchronized nervous system. All the while removing humans from the musical equation, to replace us with an algorithmic deity.

On that, as much as I would like to pull the wires out on the last two groups, I do believe it is best to slowly back out of this room. As we can now see the full process of the activation arm and its evolution — from using our sovereign energy from the earliest protest and rebellious years, to the escapism and de-individualization of humans, all the way to being built back up again as a faceless tribe, dictated to by the new algorithmic deities that have been created.

Chapter 5: The Sovereign Lineage.

January 27, 2025. I do believe I needed a couple days away to re-calibrate my mind. The two arms of music were a little intense to work through, as I could feel the hooks of the matrix reaching out, trying to suck me back in. The whole concept of the matrix; it has been the subject of many conversations over the years. “We are all in the matrix,” people say. “What our goals in life are, is to escape it.” The funny part about it is; no one can actually describe it, as they believe it is a physical state. Some people believe it is escaping the conformities of life. Some believe it is going against the government, others believe it is escaping the daily grind of life. I don’t know how many people have looked at me scornfully when I tell them I enjoy my job — that I believe job security is very important. The backlash I get — all I care about is money, or I am in the matrix. That is how an NPC lives, etc. “No, actually, I just prefer to provide security for myself.

By having a roof over my head, food on the table, and the basic utilities of life." That is not the matrix; that is wanting to lead a comfortable life.

All these people that have talked like that — they never see that the outrage matrix, or matrix, is a psychological place, it is not a physical place. It is all the psychological entrapments and snares that society has created for us, as all of the skins have shown us so far. Even materialism is a form of a psychological trap — not the part of having the basic needs in life, but the overindulgence of products the outrage matrix pushes on us.

But alas, most don't see it that way. They only see it in the way that they are shown by the very machine they say they are escaping. Just as with music, we thought we were escaping. But we never were — we were just becoming prisoners in a different way. Prisoners to an illusion, where the exit just takes us to another prison cell. Or the exit just loops us back to the main coliseum. That is why taking a bit of a break was important — not to get lost in the very mechanisms that are being mapped. As the mechanisms have been created in such a way that they are not meant to be mapped; they are meant to be hidden deep down away from everyone. In a place that no human would dare to go, so intertwined with itself that even if a person does find the mechanisms, they would find it near impossible to decipher them. Or just get lost only to find themselves back in the great chaotic coliseum.

As we look at the great coliseum of chaos from a distance, we can see and hear that it is just that — chaos, with ear-deafening noise so loud that our minds never have a chance to relax. Just as before, we can see on the ground of the coliseum the anarchy of the social media platform battles of people randomly fighting for the rented wars of others. With the great mercenary gods flying above in an endless battle for whoever pays the greatest tribute through their rituals. To the architects of the mechanics of the machine, sitting in the bleachers, watching the great scoreboard tabulating the profits harvested from the emotions of the "warriors" on the ground. We can now see at one side the stage of the sedation arm playing their engineered music to the crowds, aiming to put the audience into a state of emotional pacification. On the opposite side of the coliseum, we can now see the performance of the activation arm, blaring its wall of music upon the crowds, singing their songs of tribalism. Doing its best to whip the audience into a state of frenzy, making them feel that by losing their individual sovereignty to the hive-mind collective, they are gaining their individual sovereignty. Just all the same mechanics, just under the guise of different skins.

As we walk farther away from the deafening noise of the coliseum, a new frequency opens up as the noise fades away to silence. As we walk further away to the gates of the city that surrounds the epicenter of chaos, a bard-like noise can be faintly heard in the streets of the city. Walking to the edges of the city to the last gate, until we are back in the sovereign territory of our minds. The distinct noise of a flute becomes clearer — noise that sounds compelling yet not persuasive. Just a flute rhythmically playing in the present moment of life. Not calling or creating conflict. Nor is it trying to force us in — just playing away.

Walking down the path back to the garden, as the music grows louder. Off the path, nestled in a grove of trees, a tavern sits nestled in the trees — blending in with the surrounding trees. If not for the frequency resonating from within the walls, a person would hardly notice it is there. Just a structure built of wood and stone; the same organic structure as the music that emanates from within. The outside is rather deceitful to the actual inside — a large stage with tables and chairs all around. Large windows pulling in the natural beauty of the sun. A place where few venture, but many stay. Lost in the rhythmic sounds of the sovereign lineage of music.

The people that frequent this place are almost far and few between; they are others like us who have escaped the noise and chaos of the outrage matrix. People who, with a silent nod, know why we are here as well. Many do not talk, nor do they say where they are from. Everyone just knows — they are the others who have unsubscribed from the rented wars. Stopping at this tavern hidden away, to be lost in their internal selves as the music grounds them. Just as the flute playing, one member of the sovereign lineage plays wildly on his flute before the crowd — Jethro Tull, or I should say, Ian Anderson playing away as if the instrument was possessed by his own soul. It is a far cry from the screeching and the mental manipulations of the other arms. As his music takes on a life of its own, not asking people to subscribe to anything. Just to listen in the moment; it is like listening to a medieval bard playing away, creating a story through song and dance. Jethro Tull, as well as the other groups that perform here — they are the ones that live by a different drumbeat. They live in their own non-conformity, as they refuse to subscribe to the rented wars by refusing any cultural template.

As the bards slowly wrap up their set with the crowd giving a silent nod of appreciation for the ambiance that was created, a clock starts ticking in the silence — not loud or center stage, but in the background; just a methodical tick at first. After a minute, the ticking fades into the background. Not disappearing completely, just blending into the steady rise of a guitar tuning into the natural rhythm of the clock. As the ticking of the clock fades, the "ticking" of the guitar slowly rises to a uniform beat, almost like the beating of a heart. As the melody drifts on for minutes, it starts to create a temporal wedge in the mind, as it breaks the Pavlovian cycle of the "3-minute" pop enclosure. No immediate screaming or singing, just as the other arms. Just a slow musical buildup designed to restore the attention agency of the mind. Whereas we are no longer being fed music — we are now being asked to inhabit a space within the music. As the slow riffs of Pink Floyd roll out, slowly building to the crescendo, the faint mechanical noises can be heard; a laugh in the distance, a cash register opening, the odd scream, working into the harmonic structure of the song. Creating a structural introspection within the music, stripping away the daily grind of the machine itself. Even with the ticking of the clock, which is prevalent in the music of Pink Floyd, the music creates its own metronome.

As the vocals start to such familiar songs such as "The Wall" and "Animals," followed by navigational beacons such as the "Gilmour tone" — slow vibrato notes from a guitar that mirror the human voice — we can hear the diagnostic reality of the outrage matrix itself. All combined with the noise of the machine. The musical frequencies do show how the matrix was actually built. It is not the only group that shows us the way, or should I say, warns us about the outrage matrix itself. Some groups stand proud, demanding the silence in the room all the while living in grounded authority. Just as the late, great Nina Simone —

a very talented singer of days gone past, deeply rooted in African American spirituality and the blues.

Listening to her music, many will notice the silence she creates, pausing when the time feels right. She demonstrates to the audience that the music does not govern time, but time itself governs the music — training the listener in frequency governance, teaching the listener that we do not have to fill the void of silence with the noise of the machine. As we can stand in our own silence while we wait for the world to adjust. Even through her voice, she commands grounded authority through her contralto voice. Just as singers in the other arms use high-pitched breathy vocals that signal submission or frantic energy, her deep resonant vocal frequency signals absolute agency to the listener. Grounding the moment not in the head space of the matrix but in the gut space where our gardens are found. Living in the moment, not for the moment. In all honesty, as we sit in this little tavern at the perimeter between the outrage matrix and the garden, I could go as far as to say that Nina Simone is a steel pillar in the garden, representing a sovereign arbiter through her music. As she refused to be used by the machine, instead embracing the deep-rooted earth frequency of the blues.

Looking at the blues, or delta blues, many of the groups from the sovereign lineage draw from the concept, just as Nina Simone. In a sense, the "delta blues" are the bedrock of the sovereign lineage — a frequency of music that flows just as the Mississippi River flows and curves, ultimately leading to the Mississippi Delta itself. Is that not how the blues feels? As compared to the quantified grid of the noise from the machine? Whereas the blues play along to the heavy rhythmic thud of a boot to the floor, creating a grounding effect to the heart rate of the earth. As compared to the digital triggers of the algorithms.

With the raw jagged frequencies echoing from the hollow-body guitars and resonator noises, the high-fidelity resonance acts like a frequency cleaner to the listener, stripping away the artificial sounds of the machine.

Frequencies that the machine itself can never replicate, as the notes slide in between the standardized notes of the piano. Even in the lyrics themselves, the choice of agency stands strong — such as recognizing that the "devil" is the machine or system itself, showing the cost of engagement with the machine of the other arms. The delta blues do offer a moment of sovereign lament in the most natural way — through instruments that are played by human fingers. That truly is one thing that the other arms, through their analog and digital engineering, can never replicate: true human heart and soul in music.

The delta blues does play a key role in the musical alignment of the sovereign lineage, as other beats of the drum do as well. I have found a rather different anecdote to share. As per my job, I work with many different customers. Some I am rather indifferent to, others I have come to show a lot of respect for. This one particular customer sure likes his music — music that he plays loud enough for everyone to hear, yet quiet enough as not to become noise. The music is from our ancestral lineage, that follows low steady beats that encourage a social connection through feeling safe in a community. Integrating traditional wooden drums and ukuleles into the mix to feel like we are living on a tropical island, far, far away from the mechanical noises of the matrix. His choice of music is Hawaiian reggae music. (Something that a person would not expect in an industrial setting.) Yet the slow parasympathetic pulse of the beats does relax the atmosphere of those around, creating a rather stress-free environment to work in. A far cry from other places that constantly play music from the activation arm, where people always feel on edge and at each other's throats. It is quite remarkable when a person takes the time to see it — the influence music actually has on people. On one hand is a place that inadvertently created a frequency safe haven for the workers. On the other hand, other work environments create a high-stress atmosphere by listening to the engineered anger of the matrix itself. Even when we just ignore the noise of the frequencies, they always do resonate into our bodies.

The concept of collective sovereignty of the ancestral lineage does move on past the traditional genres or the indigenous cultures, as in the group "Can." Which is a rather unique name of a group, I must add. Nothing more, nothing less. Can acts like the organic engine, whereas the matrix uses composition as a cage to direct the listener's emotional journey. Can uses instant composition to create a living ecosystem — an ecosystem that is created in numerous ways; from the inner-space drumming, a repetitive metronomic style that adjusts in real time, thus creating fluidity, throwing aside the 808 of the matrix.

A lot of the group's songs are rhythms that are found around the world, all incorporated into an almost unidentifiable folk music. Giving us, the listener, the feeling the melodies are everywhere yet nowhere. Totally erasing the concept of tribal consolidation. Just as another sovereign aspect of the arm, the group performs in a decentralized intelligence. As no one instrument dominates, the music just emerges through the metronomic flow of the drums. Creating an improvisational flow lasting upwards of 18 minutes, breaking the 3-minute time of the music of the matrix. Where we do not feel compelled to operate on an artificial time — we start living on the river's time.

As I have stated before, we have been given warnings of the outrage matrix. Warnings that are hidden deep within lyrics, or they are the frequencies themselves. Leading us in a different direction, away from the pacifying effects or the enraging effects. There really isn't any middle ground within the outrage matrix, as it truly works on the extremes in this world. As the middle ground gives no reason for the outrage matrix to exist at all. Yet, some groups come along and give us a field report of the machine itself, while others defang the machine by simply mirroring the machine.

Just as the case with certain 1980s electro music. As much as they were showing themselves as a spectacle, they were highlighting or reporting back to us on the evolution of the outrage matrix. Just as the field linguists: the Talking Heads. They are quite the different band that certainly embraced the sovereign lineage by creating a detached analytic approach to their music. Pinpointing the mechanisms of the machine without succumbing to it themselves. Even in the lyrics that act more as code-breaking than just lyrics to a song. Almost like method-acting the matrix, the singer delivered an almost alien-like report on human panic. Acting as though he is giving a scientific report, that leaves tension in the room but not in the message itself. Even with the rhythm of African funk and world music, the Talking Heads created a map of the complex system itself. Not as chaos but as an interconnected system of the machine. Just as we are seeing right now. All the mechanics brought together in song as a field report in a form of resistant clarity. All we have to do is take time to hear the signal. Although "Psycho Killer" is quite a catchy tune, but it is always about getting back to the river.

Or sometimes the signal comes from the computer itself. I am sure by now we all have, at some point, given our computers a little "computer love." Or taking a trip down a 22-minute ride of the "Autobahn." By sterilizing the signal, Kraftwerk becomes the machine itself by creating a man-machine persona that creates linear focus for us, the listeners. By way of acoustic neutrality — of not synthesizing scary or aggressive sounds — they have created for us an acoustic neutrality in which our own thoughts can now move. Their music helps create a sense of anti-heroism, whereas the activation arm creates a tribal lightning rod. Kraftwerk moves to sterilize the noise back to pure logic, where we can now move through the great coliseum without being infected by the emotional virus of the outrage matrix.

It is kind of funny how humans acting like the machine can show us how to act within the machine. Or how the machine expects us to act within it. Yet, the sovereign lineage always finds a way around the matrix, as some groups adopted the concept of talk-sing. An interesting phenomenon that was adopted by the group "Velvet Underground." Talk-sing is rather unique in a way that it taps into the primordial aspects of our minds, where it can be viewed as the primordial cry of our ancestors — in a time where music and poetry were viewed as being together before splitting into different branches.

Talk-sing is exactly how it sounds; speaking in song where the vocals are not used as a tool for melodic rhythms, but for the phonetic sounds that are produced, where the honesty of the human voice rises over the reach for the perfect melody. Essentially creating a non-reactive transmission within the words to convey the truths of what is spoken. Voiding the activation triggers of the outrage matrix. There are groups that still practice this technique, which has been adopted more into poetry than into music.

Through the use of electric viola drones and the ostrich guitar, Velvet Underground creates a sense of harmonic stasis where the constant hum bypasses the emotional manipulation of the other arms through standard progression. Creating an unmovable frequency floor — a fixed point that allows us to observe the chaos of the world without being swept away. Even with the drumming itself, which can be viewed as anti-metronome — a drumming style that accelerates or decelerates on internal tension, as compared to a fixed grid. Mirroring the erratic pulse of the heart under pressure, showing us that time is in fact fluid and internal. Not tied to a 3-minute instance dictated by the machine. All in all, Velvet Underground is instrumental in providing structural introspection to view the world as raw, indifferent, and mechanical without being consumed by it. By now we are starting to see the patterns emerge where the whole ideal is to reclaim our time sovereignty from the artificial world. Where time is an internal fluid river, not a fixed radio clock. Whereas the concept is to bring music back to its natural flow state away from the 808 machine.

As we listen to the last set of the day within the tavern, the people silently nod in appreciation to the introspective atmosphere that drifts through the room, releasing the mind from the external. To view life internally, lost to the river of time in its natural state. Far from the prison that once shackled many. As everyone sets out back to their own gardens, the small little tavern does not look like a pub at all now, but a tower that rises above the trees. Acting as a beacon for all to see — almost like a lighthouse guiding people back to the natural flow of time. An architect that was designed by the same groups whose music plays inside. As we leave the structure for now, to continue down the tree-lined path, the natural beauty of the earth quietly fills the air; the rustle of the trees as the wisps of the wind blow through the leaves. The faint calling of an unseen animal in the distance. Feathers fluttering of a bird as it flies from branch to branch, looking for its next meal. From the insects buzzing around, even to the river not far away, with the sounds of water lapping at the shores as the water crashes over the river stone that lay just beneath the surface. As the songbirds above tweet away, as if talking to each other. Not as warnings, but as gentle banter on the backdrop of the ambiance of Mother Nature.

The ambiance we hear along the path — just Mother Nature in her totality. One would think that we as humans would embrace such earth frequencies in our lives. However, just as our busy lives dictate that we should live in rented wars, the ambient environmental music sits in the background. Not refusing to demand attention but to let us inhabit music. It is always in the background, letting us know it is there. Gently emanating from the walls as we walk through airports or malls, creating a safe place within our minds as we go about our lives. Just as always, the design is about releasing our mind from the digital time or minute-by-minute schedules of catching the next flight. Or hurrying to the next boutique, but to synchronize ourselves into our deep time. Almost like oxygen, giving us a moment to stop and breathe. As with Mother Nature herself and the earth frequencies around, there is no real beginning, middle, or end to the ambient music, with no real repetition. It creates a spectral re-wilding of the irregularities of nature to tune our ears back to the physical world. Away from the flat compression of the outrage around us.

Just as we walk along the path to our gardens, ambient music does give us an exit ramp out of the rented wars and outrage matrix. In which we can tune out the noise to enter the silence. I am not sure how many people realize that as they walk through malls and airports; the ambient music playing in the background — now we can see that it does serve a purpose by slowing us down to live in the moment of our own sovereign time. Breaking the chains of the fast-paced life we are expected to live.

As we make our way out of the grove of trees that surrounds the architecture we have just left, we can now see a safe haven away from the outrage matrix that was created through the blueprints left by Pink Floyd, in the silence and will of Nina Simone. Analyzed by the Talking Heads, through the logic of Kraftwerk. All the while being witnessed by the Velvet Underground, driven by the sounds of Can. Built on the soil of the delta blues in the ambient atmosphere of the frequencies of earth. All the while being protected by the gatekeepers that surround us. A truly remarkable place designed to protect the sovereign lineage from the outrage matrix. Just as the tower stands in the grove of trees, overlooking the land around, certain gatekeepers shine their beacons of light inward and outward, showing the paths for those who leave the coliseum on the distant horizon. Just as The Cure sits on the internal perimeter, acting as an introspective shield.

The Cure has created the ability to transcend across numerous genres, as they are viewed as electronic pop.

Many listeners view them as the Gothic type, which is not a far leap with all things considered. Through the low-to-medium melodic bass lines and the thin flanged guitar textures, they create a sense of frequency insulation for those that listen, by using colder effects that create a barrier between our nervous system and the heated effects of the outrage matrix. Just like the rest who live in the sovereign arm, the music drifts on past the 3-minute mark into minutes, following the slow unwavering drums and bass lines. Extracting the urgency out of the listener from thinking we have to be somewhere, to simply being there. Just as with the lyrics themselves — of dreams, isolation, and the passage of time — they created a sovereign way out of the matrix. "If it doesn't matter," the matrix can't use fear or status to manipulate us. In a sense, creating an existential agency by acknowledging the void within, giving us immunity against the small fears the machine harvests from us. The Cure truly stay in the grey zone by not being of bright pop colours or filled with the red anger of distortion. By providing a visual-audio neutral environment, it gives our minds a rest state where our internal gardens can begin repairing themselves.

In all honesty, The Cure acts like a shadow-work laboratory that strips away the hooks of the matrix so that we can fully enter the garden — almost like a decontamination of our minds. It is extremely ironic how such bands are picked up by a genre as with the Gothic genre, while all the time the Gothic genre are seen as outcasts of society, where they live on the fringes as the matrix does not want them. It does give a sense that the Gothic genre does see the world for what it is, with the garden being the place to be. In silence, within the noise of the rented wars. A concept that is the true threat to the outrage matrix.

As now we can see The Cure at the perimeter of the garden acting as a decontamination unit to remove the hooks from us, so we can continue on.

Other groups act as infiltrators to the machine itself. Depeche Mode did map out what we are seeing today in a form that many of us surely missed.

Just as Pink Floyd used the "mechanical" noises of everyday life, Depeche Mode adopted the same concept in their industrial phase by using recordings of pipes, hammers, and factory noise. By creating an acoustic transmutation — by taking the noises of the work prison we are all in into music — they now can perform a mechanical audit of the system, by sampling the machine and making it dance to the rhythm of humans. All the while showing us that the noises of control can be repurposed and mastered by us — the individual.

With the industrial noises themselves, Depeche Mode, through a combination of domination metaphors, spiritual and religious terminology — metaphors that represent the corporate and political power structures — use terminology to describe our internal human-to-human connections. They create a systemic transparency that strips away the master/servant dynamics that are inherent to the function of the matrix. Giving us the conceptual armour of understanding that once we see the mechanical gears of the master, we are no longer servants to it.

As with the spiritual reclamation of taking the concepts such as the divine and pulling the ideals out of the machine to be given back to us as sovereign individuals, showing that our internal gardens are accessible through ourselves, not through the priests of the rented wars — or the holy algorithms of the machine. Looking at it now, Depeche Mode can be seen as the sovereign saboteur of the machine, as their wide stereo imaging coupled with deep dark bass frequencies create analytic focus through dark space. Where every sound is cold, deliberate, and placed with precision to give an antidote to the hysteria of the outrage mechanisms.

They do show us that we can move deep into the machine to see the true wiring of the system, all the while leaving us with enough dark clarity to see the exit. Just as we have been doing as we walked through the sedation and activation arms. Once we have enough clarity to see the exit, the matrix loses its signal on us. As once we understand the mechanics inside the machine, it can no longer own us.

As we stand here now, looking around, it is becoming crystal clear that as much as the outrage matrix wants to keep us in a state of high emotion or arousal to essentially harvest our life energy, the sovereign arm does its best to relax us; to become introspective. Looking inwards to our souls, where time becomes fluid like the delta. The delta blues sits by. It is almost as if the groups of the sovereign arm know — giving us warnings while protecting the garden itself. Some groups lay on one side of the gate while others pass through to roam the coliseum, passing along the message to those who take the time to listen. Then there are others who straddle the gate — ones that lived within the matrix itself, electing to unsubscribe on their terms.

Just as the case with Led Zeppelin. I am sure at this point in our lives we have all heard a Led Zeppelin song or two. For myself, I do fancy them quite a bit as their music is easy to get lost in. Led Zeppelin is almost mystical in their lyrics of Norse mythology, a place they call "Avalon," as well as many other themes, giving way to a mythic time where it feels like I am being pulled out of the 24-hour news cycle. Into a whole different timeline, where time only exists with just the beginning and the end of a song. Led Zeppelin truly straddles the gate with one foot inside the coliseum and one foot planted firmly in the garden. Without Led Zeppelin we would not have either of the modern versions of the musical arms we see today, as they were the architects behind the activation arm back when they started, as they provided the blueprints for the "power chord" or the wall of noise that would go on to be weaponized by the matrix itself. Weaponized against us whether we know it or not.

On the other firmly planted foot; in their later years, their music became anchored in the sovereign lineage, creating the architecture that many would follow. As Led Zeppelin evolved themselves away from the power chords and the abrasiveness of the machine they were creating, they moved back to the ancestral past of mandolins and acoustic guitars, acknowledging our true sovereign lineage — one away from the mechanical noises that would become the modern-day activation arm.

Even with the other elements of the group in, say, a song like "No Quarter," they created a steady unmoving foundation through the drones of the bass. All the while being anchored biologically to the soil, from the behind-the-beat, weighted organic thud of the drummer's foot. Pulling us down into the soil of our gardens and away from the artificial world of the matrix. There are many songs to pick from in the Led Zeppelin library, such as the full 1960s version of "Moby Dick," where we get the honour of listening to John Bonham beating the drums like a man lost in his own primordial ancestry. Just beating away, lost to all concepts of digital time. I always thought that drum solo was the epitome of the drumming world. A performance unmatched by anyone else. As I watch the video, his arms move so fast that the camera cannot even keep up with him, yet the rhythm and beat flow flawlessly. He was truly an animal when it came to playing percussion, and I don't think I have ever seen another that could match his intensity except for one: Animal from The Muppets. Sure, there is no actual proof that Animal is based off of John Bonham, yet I feel that their spirit and energy are the same.

I do hold "No Quarter" in high degree as it shows the mystical custodianship of their music in full light. It does feel like a spiritual journey back in time to our true ancestral lineage, through once again singing about Norse mythology, as well as long drawn-out rhythms and a variable-speed technique of recording the song faster, then slowing the song down on playback, creating a warped, submerged frequency that feels like thick air. In a sense forming a frequency camouflage of sorts — by making it heavy and unclear, it is invisible to the activation arm's model. Forcing the listener to lean in and listen deeply, as compared to the shallow noise and engagement of the matrix itself.

Even the flow of the rhythm itself carries the weight of the song through the slow ominous 4/4 beat that makes the listener feel as if they are marching through snow; just as the vocals to the song. Far from the 808's frantic hustle pace, the march is slow and deliberate. An internal pacing whereas the messenger is not being rushed as the messenger slowly moves through the machine's territory without being rushed. The march truly is the definition of agency, all created by the rhythmic stance. The march through the snow, ice, past the dogs of doom, walking hand in hand with death, does paint that of a mystical stoicism, as the latter can be seen as the matrix. In the context we are talking about, whereas the message must get through. Metaphorically speaking, I believe it is safe to say that the howling dogs can be seen as the chaos of the coliseum without reacting towards them. Giving us an analytic anti-hysteria approach similar to what the Talking Heads would later refine — just wrapped in Led Zeppelin's mystic armour.

As with the introspective aspect, the live performances are always the way to watch such bands, as their songs tend to go from the short 3-minute trap to long improvisations, where the band just plays to the time of the music. Drifting along for 20 minutes; sometimes longer. Creating a massive non-linear experience, where time fades away. To be caught in our inner selves; lost in the frequency of the music. Almost like a beacon of our high-vibration ancestry leading us through the cold and back to the garden. I never knew at the time that I would be slowly piecing the puzzle of the sovereign lineage together through the music I listen to. Just like everyone else, I just thought it was just that — music — until I started picking up the deeper meanings and rhythms that I was listening to. Just as with the song "No Quarter." I had never heard the Led Zeppelin version before, as I had honestly thought it was an original song by Tool. It was honestly by chance that I found the song to be originally performed by Led Zeppelin. Which came as a bit of a surprise to me in a good way, as it helps to bridge the sovereign lineage across generations.

As much as Led Zeppelin can be seen as the gate to the garden, Tool can be seen as the ones who built a fortress around the gate, by securing the gate for people of the future to walk through. Listening to Tool, a person becomes immersed in the complete cognitive decoupling of the matrix itself. As the matrix does rely on the 4/4 grid rhythm to synchronize our pulses to its rhythm, Tool removes it altogether by playing in mathematical sequences. Even through the mathematical sequence of the Fibonacci sequence, such as the song Lateralus. A sequence that breaks our minds out of the forward rhythm of the matrix, by having our minds focus on the polyrhythms of the frequencies. As if one listens close to the frequencies of Tool, the rhythms are rarely in a linear path. As the frequencies almost sound like they are moving backwards, if one listens close enough. A theme that does resonate through the sovereign lineage — rhythms and frequencies that sound anti-linear, where the music feels like it is moving backwards, yet the vocals carry us forward, creating the time sovereignty that protects the garden.

That is one thing I have always noticed with the sovereign lineage of music as compared to the other arms. The flow of the music is in direct contrast to each other. As the sedation and activation arms push a person forward through the external frequencies, the sovereign arm tends to slow or stop the flow of time with frequencies that almost sound like they are playing backwards yet move forwards. Whereas the latter creates a linear motion of time, the other creates a fluid motion of time, like the ebbs and flows of the tides of the ocean. Creating fluidity in time that we can become immersed not only in the music itself, but immersed in ourselves. Complementing the silence around us. Even with the vocals of Tool, Maynard James Keenan does not sing against the music, he sings inside of it. Through his non-reactive presence within his vocals, he sings behind the music — centered and articulate. Being the calm as the frequency storm swirls around. Or others may say; the calm within the storm.

It is really systemic disruption that Tool embraces through the words that are sung themselves, through the concepts of "thinking for ourselves, questioning authority, looking at our shadow selves, even inoculation." Where we must remember to exhale and breathe, as pain is just an illusion. Where the world is an illusion and we are just an imagination of ourselves. To live in the introspective moment of the reality we have created for ourselves. Not the illusion of reality of what others expect us to live our lives in.

Not only to create deep introspection of once again songs that break the 3-minute mark, as well as songs that create a mathematical shield against the mathematically engineered frequencies of the other two arms. At this point, I am sure we can view Tool as a de-programming unit against the matrix. That is why I find the song "No Quarter" as an interesting subject. As the song No Quarter was a song originally created by Led Zeppelin, I did not realize that Tool had done it as a cover. As in a band's maturity, cover songs are usually on the rare side. That is when I came to the realization that Tool had not "covered" the song in the traditional sense as in the other arms. Whereas the cover songs are usually just a cheap gimmick to make a little extra money, that usually does not pay homage to the original band. A good example would be the shock rocker Marilyn Manson and his cover of "Sweet Dreams Are Made of These," or "I Put a Spell on You," which clearly were of the "commercial gimmick" end of things.

Yet Tool did something different with the song No Quarter. It is more of a remastering of the song than just "covering" it. By remastering the song away from the jazzy keyboard textures, to be replaced with discordant guitar gestures, it created a slow-burn breakdown that is almost nightmarish. By removing the 70s psychedelic shimmer and adding industrial friction, Tool transformed the signal of No Quarter into a defense mechanism of the digital age. Even on the vocals themselves, through the eerie detached delivery of Maynard, the focus shifts from the external "winds of Thor" to the internal "place that no one goes." Effectively moving from "mapping the terrain" to securing the internal perimeter.

Not only through the remastering and engineering of the song by preserving the sovereign drift, it reinforces the anti-hysteria shield for the more advanced, modern stages of the matrix. Not only is it unique in terms of the re-engineering, but it also shows the continuity of the sovereign signal and lineage through at least two generations. Showing us that just as the two other arms evolve, the sovereign lineage evolves as well. Or how, as much as the matrix attempts to recycle the sovereign frequency, the sovereign frequency always survives. I would not really say it is a battle between the other arms of music and the sovereign lineage. It is more of a line drawn in the sand, or as it has been put — a gate with gatekeepers protecting our sovereign time and introspection. As much as Tool creates a geometric shield around the garden, others just burn the infection that may spread across the gate. It does create a world of hurt for any of the inflicted who may try and infect the garden. An objective that Nine Inch Nails certainly takes pride in. One would not think that NIN would be a part of the sovereign lineage, but far from it. Yet NIN has its own place amongst the gatekeepers of the garden.

As we look at Nine Inch Nails, we look at the post-1994 version of them. Whereas the prior years were about pointing out the machine, the latter years represent the internal demolition and reconstruction of the machine. As the machine is loud and distorted to keep us looking at the external, NIN uses the same frequencies to launch a surgical strike on the self. Through the dynamic sovereignty of the "broken" signal — where fragility is strength — juxtaposing massive walls of distortion sounds with an extremely fragile silence, NIN uses the drop-off of the sudden silence to force us, the listener, back into our own skin. I am sure we have heard of this before, in terms of the way Nina Simone used the silence to command time and the audience, drawing them back inside. I am not sure if it is an intended lineage connection, but it is there. NIN using an evolved mechanic just as Nina Simone had used. Perhaps it is another generational connection just as Led Zeppelin and Tool?

With the sudden drop into silence, it does break the outrage loop as the listener sits in vulnerability of the quiet parts, preventing his music from falling into the aggressive trap of the activation arm. Through introspective entropy, by using glitches and decaying digital textures that are placed in the mix, NIN creates an acoustic honesty by documenting the feeling of the machine, or self, breaking down. Or in a different aspect, it shows the raw data collapse back to the anti-hysteria of the truth in which now we can see "that this is broken and we are watching it break."

In terms of internal introspection, Tool and NIN are not far apart. As with Tool looking at the shadow self and within, NIN eliminates the external other by focusing on "I, Me, My," effectively refusing the rented war by directing our energy inwards. Creating an internal architecture that makes us, the listener, immune to the tribal consolidation of the coliseum. It is pretty hard to be pulled into a rented war when we are too busy mapping the hurt inside our own machine.

When we look at the later aspects of NIN, in terms of the transition to instrumental, we can feel in the music that it mirrors the ambient gatekeepers as of earlier words yet keeping the jagged edge. It creates the final extraction, completely removing the identity of the singer, leaving only the atmospheric signal. As I said before, one would think Nine Inch Nails was in the activation arm of all places. Yet they stand firmly in the sovereignty arm. We just have to stop and listen. Just as with the song "Hurt." A song that resonates with many, not just because of NIN but from another unlikely person — Johnny Cash, who is on the other end of the spectrum from NIN in the musical genres of the world.

"Hurt," a song that uses a jarring tritone interval as well as a wall of dissonant white noise at the climax — a noise designed to be uncomfortable as to break us of the dopamine tuning of the sedation arm. NIN uses the same high-voltage tools of the activation arm to implode the ego, redirecting the rented war back onto our own internal architecture, with the ultimate question: "What have I done?"

Just as Tool removed the 70s architecture of No Quarter from Led Zeppelin's original, Johnny Cash strips the digital distortion, replacing it with his own voice weathered by his eight decades of life. All the while accompanied by his raw, creaky, wooden guitar. Through his cracked voice, Johnny Cash creates an un-engineered signal of the purest forms that the matrix can never replicate. As he moves the song totally into the sovereign lineage by singing about an "empire of dirt," he performs a complete devaluation of the coliseum. Proving at the end of life, our internal gardens are the only territory that remains.

As with the connections that have been made, I would like to point out the reciprocal hand off. Whereas No Quarter is the external defense, handed from the 1970s blueprint to the modern fortification of Tool, "Hurt" represents the internal restoration, moving the modern demolition of NIN back to the ancestral roots that Johnny Cash was. In a sense we go from ancestral to industrial. Industrial back to ancestral. Showing that the sovereign lineage is not a one-way street, but a breathing entity to move forward into complexity as in Tool, then backwards to simplicity as in Johnny Cash, maintaining the immunity of the sovereign arm.

At this point, I think I may go out on a limb and say: "So what does this all mean?" I am getting the feeling many are asking this question. So here goes: it is about using frequencies to return us to the natural flow of time and our own inner agencies. Just as the reciprocal trade between the four bands, as they are showing us that time is not linear but fluid. As well as showing us that we can use the machine's own power to protect our agency as well as reclaim our humanity. At this point, music is the social glue that holds the social glue of the outrage matrix together, as it forces us into tribal consolidation. To fight in the rented wars for others.

Through the mapping of our nervous system, the activation and sedation arm has designed itself in a way that overloads our mind so much that we eventually become sedated. To the point that we no longer look up or inwards. We just exist in the hollow structure of our bodies. As outlandish as it seems, that is the core of the outrage matrix — to have us give our life energy to it in any way possible, thereby draining us until we are incapacitated. Submitting to the digital grid frequencies that it runs off of.

It is crazy to think of such thoughts, but here we are. As I stated, being immersed in the sovereign lineage of music, we are drawn inwards to ourselves, as the musicians create an environment where time can be manipulated. To feel as if time is moving backwards and forwards at the same time, or by the changing of the heat and tempo. In which we become detached from the modern concept of time, to become reflective of our inner selves. Away from the world in which we see today. It is not just time itself. It is the introspection that is given to us as well, where we don't see the external rented wars around us. All we begin to see is that the Coliseum is built on a pile of dirt, where it has no bearings on our lives. Only when we subscribe to the rented wars does the kingdom of dirt that we create actually mean anything. It is when we start to see that the outrage matrix holds no bearing over us, does it crumble into a pile of dirt. As we begin to see that the rented wars we subscribe to only hold relevance over our lives as much as we want them to. As the outrage matrix does not have too many weapons to use against us once we start to see the machine for what it is worth. It uses frequencies to force itself into our lives, pushing as deep as it can go into our souls.

As far as I can tell, the main acoustic weapon that the machine uses against us is an obscure product called the TR-808. A relatively cheap, discontinued synthesizer from the early 1980s. A little machine that can create a 16-step process of sound that many pop and hip-hop groups use.

That loud droning bass, the perfect drumbeat all matched to a 4/4 rhythm? That would be the TR-808. An innocuous analog machine that stripped away the natural flow of the sovereign arm, replacing music with the "perfect" beats and rhythms, removing the human aspect from the musical equation.

Chapter 6: The Return to Biological Time.

Today, February 9, 2026. A new day, a new week with a new adventure in life. I would not say a new adventure, just a new day as I sit by a window with the full brightness of the early afternoon sun shining in. It is rather refreshing to feel, as it is not particularly warm out. Just warm enough to feel the heat through the window. Soon the world in the northern lands will warm, with the great glaciers of snow all around subsiding to release the ground from its frozen grips of winter, with the first signs of spring waking from the ground. It is always a time to look forward to — the return of the vibrancy of summer.

As I sit here and reflect upon what I have written; a mental break well deserved. Not as much as the intensity of the topics, but more to let not only my head but your head as well take time to digest the information, to let ourselves time to understand it all before becoming overwhelmed. Which is not what I am striving for, as that is one of the core mechanics of the outrage matrix —

to overwhelm us with sudden and large amounts of information to overwhelm our minds. To keep us in a state of constant high-intensity arousal.

I must admit that I do enjoy the silence when I give myself that — one of the main consequences of leaving the outrage matrix. Personally, I have embraced the silence or just doing nothing. Where I just let myself just "be." At this stage in my digital detox, I have now made it a habit. When I am done with my day, my evening rituals, I leave time for just myself. In which I think of things to keep myself occupied, yet the only thing my mind wants to do now is to just idle. To be left in silence with no real thoughts in my mind; just literally silence with no movement of my body. Just my whole being taking a moment to reflect or not to reflect. But to live in the moment of feeling alive, as much as that sounds like a contradiction. As in today's world, "alive" means to fill our ever-waking lives with external activities. Yet forgetting the time to feel alive by participating in internal activities.

As I have been using myself as a laboratory rat in this all after I realized that I was not going to die from the fear of missing out, I have noticed many positive improvements within myself; I feel happy, I don't feel in a rush. I feel relaxed, people around me are not as hostile anymore. I find that the flow of time has changed, as well as I feel anchored within myself. Not as being anchored in a boat upon the seas. An internal anchoring of the pillars of the foundations of a building into the ground. In a more accurate analogy, I feel that my internal source has been anchored deep into the ground. Grounding me to a different frequency, as though my internal self has grown roots that can weather any storm of the external world. It is certainly a different feeling, this whole experience of unsubscribing from the rented wars. I do know one thing: I have become extremely clear-headed and at peace with myself. People try and pull me into their rented wars once in a while. For the most part, I tell people that their opinion is valid as it is their right to have an opinion. As I have a right to agree or disagree with their opinion because in the end, it is all speculation for the most part, as most people rarely find the physical truth of what they speak of. It is just all speculation from others.

As I sit here reflecting on the past, I do have to thank my father from many years ago. If it were not for him taking me on a car ride to some stranger's place, leaving me in a parked car running in the night for a good hour, I would have never reached for the cassettes with his preferred music on them. I would never have, out of boredom, pressed play as I waited patiently for him to return to the car to drive us back home. I would have never immersed myself in the music that can now be described as the sovereign lineage. It would be music that stuck with me far into my adulthood.

As I look back now, it truly was a defining moment in my life that shaped my own musical identity. As for whatever reason at the time, the music just resonated with me. For I just felt that I could get lost in the music. As compared to the branches of the circle of friends that I hung out with — the ones who listened to pop, heavy metal, hip hop, and country. Whereas after going to gatherings where whatever music was playing, I would always go home and listen to my own music and become lost in the silence.

That was one of the great things of growing up through our youth to becoming an adult — cultivating our own personal identities. For where I was in life in my adolescent and teenage years, I was left to my own devices to find "myself." It wasn't something that was left to my parents to cultivate within me, it was something that was left to me. Just as with school in terms of joining extracurricular activities, such as sports. An activity that the school most certainly pushed in all the students. Join a sports team not for the physical activity, but to be a part of a team. To experience the pride of working with others to support the school name and alumni by winning. It was a concept I tried, but at the end of it all, I found it was not for me. It was not for the fact that I was bad at sports. The whole ideal never resonated with me. Instead, I found a different path to follow. As all my classmates eagerly joined extracurricular activities they saw fit, I found myself in the library of the school reading books.

At first I had started with literature that was geared to my own education levels. For example, in grade 7 I would read fictional books that were along the lines of the educational level I was expected to be at. Eventually evolving to more complex non-fictional books of history and reality. Leading to reading encyclopedias as well as deeper, more profound literature, such as books on the metaphysical aspects of reality. I suppose to put it into layman's terms, books on the occult or witchcraft books for lack of better terms. As I read through such literature, I came to realize that they were not fantastical, mythical concepts such as "conjuring" entities, but more of a deep, profound ideal of understanding our "true" selves. It certainly was an extremely interesting subject to read into while I was going through my youth. As all the others around me were experiencing life in their own way; creating cliques in which their lives centered around, through sports and activities. Or the ones that concentrated on their academics. I started to find solace in learning about myself, or more importantly, my inner self — that is what I had come to realize as I went through book by book, skipping over the glitz. Discovering that there were deeper, more profound ideals to life. Such as the whole concept of ego and our inner being, or ways to quiet the ego. To be at one with the universe or itself. An internal place that I learned rested inside of me. Not external.

In a sense, as I went through my education, learning about the external world of science, mathematics, social studies, and all, I found a different type of education, which employed the same principles as the traditional teachings of school. Where through mathematics, I learned about how numbers work in an internal way through concepts such as numerology. Learning a different concept of biology and chemistry through a completely different fundamental system. I am not saying that I turned myself into an occult-believing person, as I viewed the concepts and ideals from a pragmatic standpoint. As though I was looking from the outside in. The only downside to immersing myself in such literature was that it was something that I would keep internally within me. As the others my age had immersed themselves in their own lives of trading baseball cards, learning about puberty, running around chasing each other all full of hormones. Just being adolescents. The whole idea of talking about our internal selves was seen more as taboo, with the whole concepts met with ridicule and mockery. No one wanted to hear about such inner knowledge, nor did they understand it.

As time moves forward, adolescents become young adults, with priorities changing. From the pure ideals of exploring the world slowly drifting away, with playing with our imaginations through toys and games. Life began to shift for us all, as some began to take sports more seriously, identifying with their favourite sports teams as they strived to become like their idols of sports, or pushing forward with academics to achieve a spot in universities. Or just leaving school altogether, as it was seen as a waste of time, to pursue the almighty dollar of a job. The group of adolescents drifted apart. Over time, some did well in life. Some did not. I, on the other hand, had continued on my own path to a different school to finish my high school education. Once again, finding myself spending hours within a new library of infinite information. Continuing on growing the roots of my own internal identity.

As for others that I had met through my youth, internal identity was never a priority as it did not create a world around them. As creating a world inside was seen as non-constructive. When I reflect on the past now, it is easy to spot the ones that lived like that. I am not saying that there was anything wrong with them, as it is up to each and every one of us to create the life that we see fit. Yet it always seemed that it was the ones that followed the latest fads or trends of the times. Such as what bands to listen to or what sports figures to idolize. To even the types of clothes to wear. In a sense, the parts in our lives where we become introduced to the early stages of the outrage matrix. Or in a different sense, the early stages of when the hooks of the outrage matrix start reaching out to hook us. A time when we are the most vulnerable, in a sense that we are still creating not only our external identity but our internal identity as well.

It is a strange topic to bring up — the concept of the intricate, complicated ideals of identity. As it is an infinite web interconnected in so many forms, where the term of identity turns into an ambiguous word. Even from the very start; the moment in which we are born, identity comes into play. Just as in our inherited identity we receive from our parents in the form of a name — a name meant to identify us in life that becomes unique to ourselves and our personalities. For me personally, in this day and age of identifying with any and anything, I have always identified myself as my name, as it represents me. The me I have created. Even with our inherited name that sometimes is a lineage itself passed down from generation to generation. Where we are given a name or middle name that honours our older generations of grandparents or ancestors, to keep our names alive. There is also our inherited identity of our own cultures in which our families live. For some it is more profound, such as celebrating or living in the fashion of our ancestors, or how we celebrate special events throughout the year. To everyday affairs such as the rituals of eating supper, or just the overall atmosphere of how a family dynamic works. If we stop and think about it, we all experience culture in our own ways. Not as much in terms of the identification of ethnic and religious cultures. Just in the way we live within our family dynamics, which produce, in a sense, a micro-culture.

If we look at the inherited identities that we gain at birth, just as the ones that are described, I think it is safe to say that it is an identity that is not our fault. As we did not choose or earn them. We were simply born into our identities. The rest of which we create ourselves in life. Personally, it is one of the reasons that I do not feel envy for others in life. Especially when others say that person is spoiled or has it better than others. Yet I do feel pity for those that are less fortunate than others. As it seems that it is just the luck of the draw as to how we are born into this world. To be inherited by a family through our most basic concepts of identity.

As time moves on as we grow up, we start moving past our inherited identity as we begin to move into the world itself. Just as all in the world, the first ritual in life is attending school to learn. An institution that is extremely beneficial to humanity, as it helps to create an even playing field for all to learn. To become smart and intelligent; to be able to become a productive part of society when we move into adulthood. For the education system, I must say that it is a bit of a tough one. As it has evolved in many different ways over the years. Some may say that it is better today, some may not. In the context that I am speaking, it has certainly become a diverse factor in our lives. In my day it was always the core subjects for the most part. With classes that built real-life experiences for life after school, in terms of entering the workforce. Or staying at home as a provider such as home economics classes, where we learned how to cook, sew, and even how to budget household expenses. That was as diverse as school got when I was growing up, with the only real imposed identity being school pride. Through once again, sports games against other schools.

Seeing the evolution of the education system over the years, it does seem as though it has turned into the starting point of our self-imposed identities that follow us through life. Whereas we come to externalize our identities to fit in with the groups around us. Sure, a person can be great at whatever activity they choose, but fitting in with the crowd is just as important as well. Or so we are told; whereas to be a team member, we must give up our individuality for the good of the team, to become a collective entity. Fighting on the field as not just one, but as all. In a way that we are told that we must don jerseys of our schools as that is what our identities are about. In a sense, teaching us that just as the activation arm of music. That in order to be a part of a group, we must join the concept of tribal consolidation. Where we are taught the ideals of the rented war, as we are not playing sports or being involved in other extracurricular activities for the pleasure of learning something new. We become fighters, as we must win the “battle” to boost school spirit. Looking at the ideal of school spirit. In its pure form, it is a great concept to teach children, as it creates a sense of pride that goes on later to create a sense of community and national pride — to be proud to be a part of the larger collective. Seen as our national identities, depending where a person lives. Which, depending on how a person sees it, can be a good thing or a bad thing in terms of the political skin.

As we grow past the external identity that builds upon “school identity,” the scaffolding does build up in other different aspects, in terms of external identity. Whereas we are taught different ideologies of how to live, what to believe, what political party to follow. As we learn about different forms of politics, in which we find that we should identify with a particular political ideology. In a sense not as the term “identity” itself, but in terms of what political structures resonate with us. In terms of the direction we want to see the world go. I do believe that description is more suited for the context we are talking about. As all political structures are flawed; we are trying to pick the best out of the flaws. In looking at the ideal of identifying with a particular political system over another.

Although school pride can be seen as one of the building blocks of our external identities as we grow into adults, there are other underlying or hidden aspects of the growth of our external identities, as almost everything we do throughout our times in educational institutions — even into college or university — are the scaffolding to hold us up. Even the concept of grades, which is extremely important to evaluate how we are progressing, can be seen as a piece of the scaffolding as well.

As it does create yet another means in which we are identifying with the system, in terms of where our places will be when we get older. Just as the social groups that are created, that become important as we move into secondary education. Whereas we join fraternities or groups that share the same educational interests. Whereas we all feel the need to “fit in” with the collective identity of whatever groups we are compelled to join.

As we look to feel accepted with different groups, we are compelled to fit in. Are we not? Where we see different tribes that we would like to be a part of, yet we conform ourselves in one way or fashion so as to be accepted by the tribe itself, giving up a part of our internal identities to be accepted. Looking at it all now, it certainly does go beyond our educational years to follow us into the workforce.

I am not sure if anyone has ever heard this line before: “you have the skills for the job. It is all a matter if you fit in with the other workers.” I have heard that one many times in my life. Whereas the internal structure and identity I have created, by honing my skill sets, are always secondary to creating a new external identity to fit in with a group. In which, if the group doesn’t like me, the job doesn’t last too long. As it is truly never about the skill sets, it is about “fitting in.”

So, our external identity is never secondary to our internal identity in the world. It is always at the forefront. It is as though the system has been set up in that fashion; to build ourselves up with the scaffolding of external validation from a group to create our identities. A scaffolding system that sways in the winds, that can give way, threatening the whole structure of our external identities. There is balance that can be found. Such as in a term I have read and heard numerous times from sources all over: "As above, so below." A term that many have stated that ends up ambiguous, as the phrase is so vague it could mean many things. For the most part, it seemed to be a phrase about how we see ourselves in a mirror, or our reflection as to how we present ourselves in the world. Which can be seen as an accurate depiction. But at this point I must add, I don't want to sound like I am drifting off into the spiritual guru skin. In the architectural context of what I am explaining, the phrase does appear to hold relevance.

It is quite the concept of using a tree as an analogy for our identities, oddly enough. Humans have used a tree as an analogy to life numerous times over the centuries. In this context we can view ourselves as a tree at various stages of growth. As when we are born, we are just a seed that is planted in the ground with only our inherited identities. Just like the genome of a seed itself; all of the fundamental building blocks are there that "make us who we are." As our seed germinates, roots start reaching out into the soil.

As we learn who we are and what we are — we begin to think with our own minds. Learning not of the outside world, but as much of our inside world. Of using our senses to hear, see, taste, and think. Internalizing our external world. To be able to identify the outside world; the basic building blocks of our world.

As our seedlings grow into saplings, the trunk branches out to grow the leaves of our external selves. All the while being fed by our roots that grow in the soil of life. As our tree grows in the world, our trunk grows larger, branching out in different directions. Just as our external identities branch out, through the ways that we are compartmentalized into different groups by the institutions of life. Or in a different context, the environment around us which creates the growth of our external trees.

An environment that can create an artificial growth of our external trees, by propping us up through the engagement of others. Just as we are propped up to become a part of groups to fit in. An artificial growth that leads us to believe that identity comes from tying ourselves in with groups that we think share the same morals and values. In which our life becomes validated by others to lead us to believe we are organically growing. All the while, as we artificially grow our external identities, we begin to neglect our inner identities. Our roots — the part of ourselves that is responsible for creating our morality in the world. Such as our moral compass as to what is right or wrong. The establishment of our own personalities and beliefs away from the collective environment that our trees inhabit.

As we push to "fit in," to join different tribes, it appears that our moral compasses are the first to become neglected in our root system of our trees. As being an individual going against a tribe always leads to animosity and ultimately being condemned from the tribe. As much as we like to think that we are an individual in a tribe, we always end up conforming in some fashion — giving up a part of our internal identity. Which leads to the roots of our trees suffering. We may not think much of it. As we neglect the roots of ourselves, we start to build a scaffolding around our external trees to prop ourselves up in the world through the validation of others. Through looking for compliments. Being acknowledged for the work we do, applauded for winning a game; even getting likes and engagements on social media. A scaffolding system designed by the machine to keep our external trees growing in any environment that it is in. Leading us to believe that the trunk, branches, and leaves of our trees are healthy and flourishing. Sadly, it seems to be a concept that society has graciously picked up to be taught in every institution in our lives. It is almost like a fundamental building block of society. To build us up by the scaffolding of society.

As with life, we are always frequented by storms that hit our trees. Not as in the literal sense but in a metaphorical sense. Such as failing a course after being propped up that one was passing. Being cut from a sports team after being praised for being sportsmanlike. Getting fired from a job after passing a review with flying colours. As the scaffolding that the world has given us turns out to be weak in the face of the storms of life-changing moments. Pillars that appeared strong because of the words of others turn out to be weak and brittle in the world. Not being able to hold up our external trees, as the world has shown us that we can still grow and neglect the roots of our internal selves. The part of us that says it is okay to fail, it is okay to be wrong, it is okay to lose a job. As it is not us that caused the failing, it was caused by life showing us that there is a lesson to be learned. A lesson that can come in many different forms; maybe sports was not for the person in the long run? Or maybe a person needed to learn a little more before progressing? Maybe the job was not where a person was meant to be for long? All questions and ideals that come from our roots, to create strong foundations inside of us to be able to handle the storms, to hold us grounded to the world. As not to have our external trees buckle under the weight of the relentless winds of life.

I am sure we have all been in a situation where we have so-called failed at an endeavor. In which we stop and think why and how it happened. Some of us may just rationalize things then move on with life. Some of us may feel the collapse of the scaffolding around our trees. In which the validation is gone, to see that the roots cannot support the tree. Ultimately lashing out at whoever threatens their external identity that has been built. Looking at the events of the world, it does feel that way — that the world decided to build us up through the concepts of external identities so that we become a de-individualized collective of people. In a way it feels as though, to keep on feeding the outrage matrix. Whereas having us create a brittle scaffolding around us, when our scaffolding is threatened or damaged in any sort of way, we lash out at anyone and anything, as it feels a threat to our existence.

Just as the outrage matrix feeds upon our negative emotions, it forces us to abandon our internal roots. As a tree with deeply rooted foundations can never be blown over by the storm. No matter how relentless the winds may be. We may bend and sway, yet we will never buckle and break as our own personal resolve is insurmountably strong. As the winds blow through when our roots are shallow with the scaffolding holding our trees up, the winds of life begin to knock down little bits here and there until the trunk starts being exposed. Effectively creating a fragmentation of external identity, making us feel like our whole world is literally falling apart around us. Creating anxiety and hostility inside of us against those who force the storms upon us. Lashing out in rage and anger on how the world could do this. Ultimately leading to violence with some. Taking it to the ultimate extreme; killing others and themselves in a last-ditch effort to defend what they see as their crumbling worlds. An energy and design that is, unfortunately, the ultimate feast for the outrage matrix.

There is no reason for the world to be set up on such ideals, as we should look first at the fundamental building blocks of our own root systems first. An ideal that should be instilled in all of us in our youth. When we see an agitated child; we are always told to give them something to do to keep them occupied. Maybe though, they are just going through their own internal growing pains of their own roots? Same as a brooding adolescent, we give them medications and such to correct the behaviours. Yet perhaps those behaviours are once again the growing pains of their own roots? Or perhaps they are taking the time to do the painful process of pruning their external branches to remove the deadfall. To allow new branches of growth to happen, above the ground just as below?

That to me is an ideal we should all look at from time to time. Just as weeding the unwanted from a garden to let the wanted grow. Taking the time to prune our external trees so that the weight of the branches does not force us to prop ourselves up through an artificial structure around it. Allowing our roots to adjust and grow accordingly. It may sound like a wild concept, yet at the end of it all, it is about focusing on ourselves to realize that we do not need to rely on external validations or conforming to fit in with groups of others. It is relying on internal validations to know in our hearts that we have the moral compass to know which direction in life to go in. To be able to handle the storms of life through our own internal resilience and strengths. Where the only fitting in we have to do, is fit in with ourselves.

As much as it may sound like I am hinting that we all should become reclusive, or shun away from the idea that we should not become a part of groups or society, as it helps to foster an artificial, external identity of ourselves — in which identity is no longer a name but a description of us — that is not the case. It is about having individual sovereignty over our identities in which we have full internal control of it. All the while maintaining our social presence in the world. Just as a forest of healthy trees that communicate through their root systems and canopies that thrive in an ecosystem together, as compared to a bouquet of flowers that all look the same. Plucked from their roots, to be placed in a vase. Already dying as they have been severed from their roots.

"As above, so below." As we grow older with a balance in our trees, between our roots and the canopy, the ideals and identities of our roots become the identities of our canopies. As the external identity of our canopies becomes buried in our roots. As we grow in the currents of time, carried forward whether we're ready or not. A leaf falling from the canopy doesn't choose its path, and in many ways neither do we as we move from adolescence into adulthood. We prepare for years, yet when the moment arrives, we're suddenly faced with a world that feels larger and more demanding than expected. Every decision now rests on us alone.

Even with all the preparation of our youth, it's fair to ask whether we're ever truly ready. Most of what we're taught equips us to survive whatever storms come our way, but not always to understand ourselves. That's why building an internal identity early on matters so much. Those roots become the foundation we rely on long into adulthood. Leaving our childhood homes for the first time shows us how big the world really is. Not necessarily frightening — just unfamiliar. For the first time, every choice is ours: where to live, how to work, how to support ourselves. These decisions shape the direction our lives take.

Education pushes us toward a career, asking us to invest our time and skills into a role we hope will fit. Some people find their "dream job" right away; others move through several before something aligns. Either way, the transition is the same. We trade chalkboards for presentations, extracurricular activities for overtime, and childhood routines for the responsibilities of adult life. Yet the environment still echoes the systems we grew up in. Workplaces often recreate the same external identity pressures we learned as kids. We're encouraged to fit in, to adopt the "spirit" of the company, to see competitors as rivals. Conformity becomes the price of belonging. Being a "yes" person is treated as maturity. Questioning is discouraged. We're expected to perform without friction, sometimes to the point of being seen as more mechanical than human.

Maybe that's why our early institutions focused so heavily on external identity — it's easier to manage people who rely on external validation. Praise, promotions, and approval become the currency of belonging. But internal identity doesn't grow from that. Sovereignty comes from the ability to think, to discern, to act from one's own center rather than from fear of stepping out of line. I've experienced this tension in my own career. I've often been placed in roles where I'm expected to do the job without asking questions. But my work is dangerous enough that unthinking obedience can cost lives. Sovereignty isn't rebellion — it's responsibility. It's using my judgment to keep myself and others safe. I've seen what happens when people silence their internal compass just to satisfy external demands. One wrong move can change everything.

This dynamic shows up in less hazardous jobs too. People are told to hide mistakes, ignore wrongdoing, or look the other way because "that's how things are done." Anyone who refuses becomes labeled a problem — a whistle blower, a snitch — when in truth they're simply following their moral compass. In the end, it comes down to the difference between engagement and enmeshment. Healthy workplaces create connections and autonomy, like a forest where each tree stands strong on its own roots. Dysfunctional ones blur boundaries, demand compliance, and erode identity until people feel defined by the group instead of contributing to it.

But alas, as the river of time flows forward. In spots it flows deep and slow, with other areas flowing shallow and fast. As we are just leaves floating on the surface, going in whichever way the current takes us. A leaf that has gently floated down from the canopy of trees above. Just as with our own trees in life. Time goes by as we grow from adolescents into adults. Faced with a whole new world in which we learn to adapt to the "adult" world that lies before us. A world that we spend most of our youth growing up for, just as with our inner trees as we reach maturity. A point in our lives when we truly become the masters of our destinies, as now all the decisions that we make rely on us and us alone.

As much as we are prepared for our adult lives, are we truly prepared? Or taught just enough to be able to survive whatever storm may come our ways? For the most part, I personally want to say yes. Although there is always the uncertainty of what life can throw at us. That is why it seems that building our own internal identity through our roots is so crucial in our youth. As it provides the foundation to survive long into our adulthood. As we move on from our families; to leave our childhood homes for the first time, we truly learn how big the world truly is. I would not say scary, as that concept is all about perspective.

Whereas for the first time in our lives, all the decisions we make fall squarely on us. Decisions such as finding a career, a place to live, finding food, and paying our ways in life. Decisions that will ultimately lead to which direction we go in life.

As the educational institutions of our past have demanded, the biggest decisions we make is of course a career in which the skill sets that we honed throughout our time in the education systems are now put into practical use. As picking the proper education to fill a "spot" in the workforce is an educated guess where we invest our lives into the speculation that our hard work and perseverance pays off. Some will luck out and find their "dream job" on the first try, whilst others may move through many jobs to find their "dream jobs." Thus, we make the transition — we switch chalkboards for PowerPoint presentations. We switch extracurricular activities for overtime and board meetings. We switch sports equipment for power tools. Yet the environment still holds close to the environment of our trees that grew through our youth.

An environmental ideal that once again focuses on the growth of our external identity of fitting in with coworkers and adopting the "spirit" of the company that we become employed with. Whereas the competing companies are just that — competition not for academics, but for economic survival. Where we once again become a part of a tribe where we see other tribal companies as a hostile threat to our own tribe's existence. It is where we learn the ultimate form of conformity of fitting in or being kicked out. Creating an environment where toeing the line by being a "yes" person is tantamount to being a sovereign adult. I am sure we have at some point in our lives ended up in that position. Or will end up in that position where we are expected to externally conform to the company. Where we are expected to earn our paycheques by just doing our jobs, with no questions asked. As the whole idea is to just perform, to the point that we are seen as robots more than sovereign humans in the world.

Perhaps that is why the institutions of our youth focus so much on our external identities over our internal identities? As it is easier to manage us when we are always seeking external validations such as a commendation for a job well done. Or a promotion or raise for following the line. As compared to having sovereign humans that can look to their internal identities to guide them through what is right or wrong. To be innovative and unique where we do not seek external validation through just "performing" well at our jobs, but by seeking internal validation of just "creating" for a company.

(An ideal that many despise in a corporate ladder, as it breaks the chain of command through non-conformity. How do you keep a person in line if they are not seeking a promotion or raise? They are just working for their own internal benefits?)

It is an ideal that I have come to know rather too well. Being a "yes" person instead of being a thinking person. As in my own career, the people that are in charge always put me in a position where I am not supposed to ask questions. I am supposed to just do or perform with no questions asked. A line of thinking that runs contrary to my own sovereign beliefs. Not as much as being insubordinate, but along the lines of using my own internal identity as a sovereign person to keep myself alive. With keeping people around me safe as well — a concept that is always missed by the middleman in the companies I work for. They just expect a job to be done, and don't think for myself. Yet, if I were not to use my better judgment or to rely on my inner judgment, people do get hurt, or worse. I have seen it many times in my days — one wrong move and things can turn tragic in the blink of an eye. All because we are expected to perform, with no individual thinking.

In a sense, we are expected to just leave our moral compasses at home. Locked deep within our roots, as to not interfere with the flow of the corporate order. Yet time and time again, I always stand strong to my words and actions. As I cannot be fired or looked down upon for not crumbling under the peer pressures of others. To put myself or others in harm. It is certainly not external validation that I am looking for, it's just my own deeply rooted beliefs that we all must go home the same way we showed up to work. Just a little bit wiser. That is my own experience, as my line of work can be extremely hazardous where in a split second all can go wrong. It is no different from the jobs that others have in terms of being sovereign adults where the internal identity of our roots leads us. Just as a person is told to hide mistakes on ledgers, or look the other way when people are doing injustices, such as stealing. Or just acting in nefarious ways where we are supposed to "go along" with it as it is just normal business practices. Where by calling out such practices, we are "identified" as a whistle blower or a snitch. When in all honesty, we are just following our moral compasses.

I suppose in reality in terms of employment; it comes down to the difference between engagement and enmeshment. Where working with a team of coworkers is about creating a healthy supportive atmosphere that creates connected relationships and autonomy. That allows the environment to thrive on its own, just as a forest of healthy trees thrive together. As compared to a dysfunctional, codependent dynamic of micromanaging and external oversights that blur the boundaries of our job titles, creating a sense of lost identity. Just as a bouquet of flowers as we are pushed to be defined by a group, instead of joining a group.

Community identity — it is a strong force that lies beneath the surface of our lives. No matter where we go, the identity is always there in one shape or form. As outsiders to a new community, we can always see the local norms and expectations. Where there are unspoken rules of values, behaviour, and belonging. These identities are usually invisible to the ones inside of the communities, yet to an outsider the identity of a community becomes quite obvious. Looking outside into a community, a collective persona is typically seen. Whereas our sovereign self can come to odds with the community — if the matrix cannot harvest us as an individual, it will try to harvest us as a component of a group.

Looking at the concept of a community, we can look back at the frequencies of music. Mainly the activation arm, as a community can be seen as a distributing network of that particular arm. To start, to even become a part of a community, we are expected to tune ourselves into the frequency of the collective persona. A community frequency that to pay the admission, we must give a small part of our internal identity to adopt the labels and outrages of that community. In a sense, if the collective persona of the community is tuned into the outrage matrix, we end up subscribing to the matrix through the proxy of others, where their rented wars become ours. As we enter a new community, our identities meet one of the real tests in life. As the collective persona of a community can be seen as another form of tribal harvesting through herd mentality. Through entrainment, a herd mentality stands. In which the collective persona of the community tries to overwrite our quiet selves through manipulation. A feedback loop where the members of the community act as internal wardens for each other. A feedback loop where if we stop wearing the labels and unsubscribe from their rented wars, the community will often attack one who has a non-reactive stance.

There is a sovereign alternative to the activation arm of the collective persona of a community. An alternative that can be described as a resonant proximity towards each other. An ideal that shares no persona, in which we are all our own identities. Just as the mature trees of a forest, each sovereign to their own roots. Yet still quietly communicating just as the people who sat in the tavern. Gently nodding their head in approval to the bands that played upon the stage — a silent nod of the head. Or a handshake with one of similar frequencies, always acknowledged in silence. A sovereign community that has no central hub or rented wars to share. They are just off the grid of the outrage matrix as a community should be defined by what we do in the community — not the community defining who we are. Even when we try to be our quiet selves within a community, the matrix always pushes back. As being non-reactive or "indifferent" is seen as a threat to the machine. In terms of being indifferent, which is one of the biggest shields against the outrage matrix, as well as one of the biggest weapons against unsubscribing from the rented wars. The indifference lies in being emotionally non-reactive to the triggers of the machine. As compared to the beliefs that “indifference” is a sign of apathy or weakness — as described by some who are shackled in the prisons of the outrage matrix.

This can be seen as the first real test of our internal sovereignty and identities, as to “fit in” we must resonate with the collective persona’s specific rented war. By trying to hook us through emotional manipulation. Whereas if we react, the community generally accepts us. Or we are rejected because of our indifference. At this point, it becomes an extraction point to dilute our identities. To have our identities merge with the collective. To have our internal energy rerouted from ourselves to powering the community’s narrative. Once again; when we stop saying “I am” and start saying “we are,” we lose our internal identities to the collective external identity. With one of the passing grades of having the ability to be in a room of screaming people while remaining silent to the noise around us. Where we look at ourselves as a guest or an observer, not as an actively subscribed member. By staying true to our internal identities, one must look at every statement with the word “we” in it. If “we” are expected to abandon our internal borders in such statements, possibly it is time to reassess the situation.

As for now, looking at a community; it can be seen as a grounding force that shapes us by reinforcing our internal identities as well as growing our external identities. Or it can be seen as a distortion by the matrix, through social pressure. We must synchronize ourselves to the collective, effectively distorting our internal identities to match the common rented war. Looking at ourselves in a community, one does have to identify the “lean” factor. A factor that determines what kind of community one is involved in, as the concept does push two different paths. One of the sovereign lean, to which the community supports our internal borders. A feeling where we tend to feel heavier as we are grounded to our own identities. Or the lean towards the matrix in terms of feeling lighter as our internal borders become accessible to others. Giving a light feeling of anxiousness as ourselves are being bent away from our internal identity, where it fractures into the distributed network of the activation arm. All the while creating a healthy or unhealthy environment.

Joining a community lies within our biological necessity of wanting to belong to a group for safety reasons. Just as our primal tribes grouped together millennia ago — to protect ourselves from danger all the while working in the tribes. A biological safety signal the environment signals to us that we are indeed in a safe place, lowering our fight-or-flight responses to induce our safety mechanisms of relaxation and healing. The result is that people find themselves amongst others that feel and act the same way, as if all are resonating on the same frequencies in the world. Just as the healthy forest of trees; independent yet standing together to weather the worst of storms.

On the other side of the coin, we have merging with a community. In a sense that a person loses their internal identity to fuse with the collective identity. Erasing our own balance of sovereignty which makes us ungovernable, to become a part of the machine. From going from "you are here and I am here" to "there is only us." To where we must think: are we part of a collective persona? Or do we belong in the garden? Do we reach out to take each other's hands in belonging? Or do we fist-fight or hug each other into a merging suffocation of blurred borders?

Just as with all concepts and ideals of life, identity is not static just as a photograph. It is dynamic as it reveals its strength from the environmental stresses of the storms of life. As the branches of a tree sway and bend in the winds yet never break and snap. A true sign of the strength of our internal identities, away from the brittleness of the external scaffoldings. At this point, we can view the environment as a diagnostic tool. Just as standing in the great coliseum of chaos, surrounded by the noises of the activation arm, listening to the fever-pitched screams. Or the cries of the outrage crowd to the point a person feels empty. Ultimately subscribing to the outrage from feeling empty from looking for who a person is in the outrage matrix. Only to see a fragmented victim of who one was.

As where sitting in silence of the tavern listening to kind, drawn-out riffs of the sovereign environment. Breaking away from the external noise of the coliseum, to look introspectively at ourselves. Feeling a heavy groundedness of our quiet selves. A place where we see in the silence who we are as sovereign identities. Either which way, the who or identity that we become turns into the output of energy into the world. Where the sovereign identity turns into not letting the noise define an identity; but to let the identity define the room. Through sovereign support, a healthy community thrives without the need to fit in or the erasure of the internal identity. A concept that draws its strength from the individuality of the collective. In a sense where one individual decides to be silent or non-reactive, or changes their identity, the rest of the collective remains stable as the respect of each individual's internal identity is upheld. Creating essentially a safe place for our identities to rest. Instead of a constant feeling of defending against tribal activation due to the demand of the total synchronization of the collective persona. A synchronization that is demanded in an unhealthy community, as if a person does not merge completely with the collective persona, the system starts to break, pushing for all to conform to the specific ideals and external identity of the community. A system that views being a sovereign identity as a breakdown that can only be repaired through shaming or cancellation. Effectively guaranteeing compliance and conformity within the community.

This all does create a break in the system, or diverging paths. As now silence becomes the armor as well as the weapon, depending on how one looks at it. The silence as armor starts to emerge from the ideal that our quiet selves lead to our sovereign selves in a room full of noise. Effectively blocking out the frequencies of the outrage matrix, providing internal strength to our identities. In a healthy community, silence is seen as an asset. In an unhealthy community, silence is seen as a weapon. In a sense that silence is seen as dissent or a failure to engage, as to remain silent is a breach of the collective persona. As silence does not have room in the noise of the rented war's outrage — a reason why we are taught by the machine that silence must be avoided at all costs. As silence creates a strong individual living in an unharvestable group. In which the community's health relies on the unsubscription of its inhabitants.

Keeping with the unhealthy community, it can be seen as a mass-production factory. As it does not want sovereign individuals, it wants a unit just as with a military unit. In these environments, identity is converted away from the internal identity into a visual and linguistic costume. Not as much as physical clothing but in the context of approved labels, vocabulary, and synchronized behaviours. All following the approved narratives of the single leader of the collective persona, in which we pay a membership fee from our own internal identity. To always stand up and defend or fight for the group's rented wars, just as with gangs. They wear the same clothes, speak in the same vocabulary, and act in the same way. All as a unit, taking orders from the leader to which individuality is looked down upon. A permanent membership to another's wars, creating a subscription model that one can never cancel. Just as with the military itself; can a person disagree with the orders given to them? Or will they be reprimanded for insubordination by the others in the tribe?

Sovereignty within a community is our ability to stay to ourselves as we stand with others. Sovereignty at this point can be seen as a refusal to entrain ourselves to be colonized by the collective noise of others while standing with our own internal sovereignty of our identities. In a way that resonates through us. Or more importantly resonates with others around, in a sense that if one person is high-stressed, the rest in the room become high-stressed. Where it is up to us to be empathetic as others react emotionally. By becoming an anchor in a time when the community is pushing for activation through validation or outrage. A person must be empathetic towards those around in terms of their own external identities. Looking at it from another's perspective, to not fall into the reactivity trap of the outrage matrix. Certainly aspects do emerge from a person that is subscribed to the collective persona's rented wars. As their voice may crack, or hesitations, or just a general weariness.

For it is not each other that are the enemies but the machinery of identity capture that turns us against each other through tribal consolidation. As we all do have a biological need to be a part of a community, yet it is our quiet self that reinforces our internal and external identities. To become standing waves in a field of oscillating noise. As in becoming empathetic to the true human that is caught in the collective persona of a community, it is worth noting that they have been caught in the machinery of identity capture as well. Whereas standing in our own quiet silence, the frequency will resonate from within to others, washing over others to silence the room from the noise of the outrage. We all become passionate towards the identities that we create for us, as that is the life force within us — the sap that flows through the tree. To create ourselves in a way in which we feel alive, as that is all that truly matters in this world. Is to be alive.

In terms of identity within a collective persona, the matrix wants us in one of two states. To merge our identities to the point that we do not have an internal identity at all — just an external identity, held up by a brittle structure. Or total isolation, as to not live within a community at all. Whereas sovereignty is the third way by maintaining our internal roots of our identity, all the while still being a part of the social structure. In a sense of creating a Faraday cage through indifference. As being indifferent shields our internal frequencies and identity from the social signals sent out by the community. To hit our own external personas yet never penetrate into our internal personas. Putting us in a position to exchange information and resources in a community, all the while shielding us from merging our identities. Essentially creating an anchor for ourselves as we see our own validations within us trumping the external validations of the matrix. Giving us a deeper internal structural compass to guide us through the collective persona of the community. Effectively creating a breaker that we can pull any time to remove ourselves from the noise. Empathetically moving us towards being a functional asset in the community. By returning back to the original of a community through physical protection and work through our passionate instincts of belonging. Denying the community access to our internal roots and identity through indifference when the collective persona activates its subscriptions to its rented wars.

Chapter 7: Time Sovereignty.

I do believe it is February 17, 2026. As I sit here staring at the frozen lands of the world, buried in feet of snow from the blizzard that blew through the night before, leaving a vast winter wasteland in its path as people scramble to dig themselves out so as to make their morning commutes to work. Just as the rest, I was out early as well, shoveling and digging so as not to fall behind in my deadline to make it to work on time. It is a minor inconvenience in life — the winter months. Yet it creates a certain degree of time management, as life just takes a little longer than the summer months.

As the world digs itself out this morning, there is not much to do except wait. For the world to start working again; for customers to come by; to begin another day. Sometimes the wait is the hard part, as time feels like it has slowed to a crawl. Far from the busy days that have passed, where time feels like it flies by, rarely slowing down for a person to take a break — to stop and take a breath in life.

Time is a concept that can be elusive as well as deceptive in terms of how we perceive it. It acts like the dynamics of a river, as at some points it can become as still as the waters of a lake, or it can push forward so fast that it creates rapids crashing upon the rocks the water pushes over. In other moments, time can feel like it is moving in reverse, just as the back eddies formed on the edges of the river, ultimately circling around to flow down the river.

Just as with the dynamics of the river, time can act multifaceted in a way that, as much as it can be perceived as a river in the mind, in the background a clock slowly ticks away. Counting the seconds in a steady rhythm that never changes. Just a tick, tick, tick, as seconds pass turning into minutes, eventually hours into days. It is a raw energy that is never seen and barely felt as it just sits there in the background. A raw energy that creates the whole world around us, as without time we would cease to exist.

Time is the true currency in life. A currency more valuable than any other, as it is the only resource to us that can never be regenerated. An energy that starts the moment we are born, before our identities are even created. It is a currency that is stolen from us all the time in our lives, just as in the digital world itself. In a way, through the design of creating short content of 15–30 second videos designed to fragment our attention to harvest our time. Trading our time currency for the convenience of the internet or the validations we look for. Ultimately creating a "clock tax" that taxes our own existence from the constant notifications of our social media we immerse ourselves in.

Just as with every ping of our devices which demands a "now" response — a temporal levy — that full attention is given just to pay with our time.

As we look at time from a sovereign standpoint, time could be seen as a stored potential. In a sense, as a battery. Whereas tuning to the outrage matrix, time is spent living in the regrets of the past or the anxiety of the future; slowly draining our energy or time. As viewing time as a battery in the present time, time can be used to charge the battery to maintain our internal territory. Refusing to use our time energy as a commodity, we can become tax exempt as we can own our own chronology.

The world has been set up in a gear that only sees overdrive as the answer, as compared to the older days of running on cruise control. Where everything has a sense of urgency to it; the notifications, headlines, even the way people speak. In a fast, hurried tempo that demands attention now. A world created by the outrage matrix to steal the one real currency we have — time.

As with the musical activation arm, the machine does use frequency entrainment to override our own biological clocks through high-frequency noise. Just as the 808 grid or high-speed synthetic beats per minute override our natural frequencies. The machine uses the high-frequency arousal of the 24/7 news cycle, short-form videos, and instant demands to throw our brains out of our alpha/theta waves of quietness and creativity into high-beta states of reactivity and panic. Creating micro spikes of notifications, all to overclock our internal tempo so we always feel the need to check and react, even when there is no threat to us.

The temporal fragmentation makes it impossible for us to focus on our internal clarity, as our focus is broken every 30–45 seconds, which keeps us out of the true present. Giving us a temporal poverty that we desperately fill with the quick-fix rewards of the activation arm. Just as the sovereign lineage of music that uses long-form drift as a template, it is an effect that can draw us out of the temporal fragmentation, back to lengthening our focus. Essentially taking the time to draw a long breath. Unless one has a deadline to meet.

"A line that is fatal to cross," or a deadline that many if not all of us have run into in life. A psychological deadline artificially designed to create a high-panic state, forcing us to abandon our inner clarity for speed and reaction — a continuous stress loop used on us to sacrifice our internal selves for the external demand of others. Leading to a high-output situation where we become the "yes" person in the chain. Giving up our own sovereignty to conform to the collective persona. In which tempo is used to take our time energy away. We become dependent on the matrix clock, away from our biological clock as the tempo is increased by the matrix.

All the while, if we ask who sets the tempo? We can replace the "deadline" with our biological completion, as we will meet the "deadline" just on our own time by refusing the "urgency" of the signal.

As the tempo increases, our internal rhythm decreases, leading to the collapse of our internal rhythm. As we stop resonating to our internal clocks and start resonating and mimicking the clock of the matrix. By staying in the chronic activation state of outrage and fear, our heart rate variability falls into a chaotic, incoherent pattern. Even with the grid pattern of the 808, just as in the activation arm, we become bombarded with a constant danger signal. A danger signal that breaks our long-form drift of thought. Fragmenting our minds into the loss of judgment as we see motion as progress, not progress as motion.

Pushing ourselves to become reactive in nature, away from the slow intentional motion of our biological clock. A situation that, even in the stillness of silence, we feel rushed as we lose the ability to rest, reflect, or choose in life. In a sense, the matrix makes us too fast and noisy for us to look at our internal roots of deep introspection, where our minds become too noisy to stop and become sovereign.

To look at my own speculations: just as the musical arm uses frequencies to illicit a response from our neurological and biological systems by bypassing our bodies to trigger a chemical flooding of dopamine and cortisol, having an adverse effect on our physical health in numerous different ways, my own speculation is: are many neurological diseases such as attention, memory, and other cognitive disorders caused by the temporal fragmentation created by the artificial time that we are forced to live by? As we have been put into a system that does not allow us to run off our own biological clocks and internal rhythms?

It is hard to say, as it is all just a theoretical concept that is not backed by any scientific principles. It just seems the picture being painted starts to reveal that subjective opinion of our fast-paced lives we lead.

It almost feels that the faster we go, our internal selves begin to disintegrate in the heat of the friction that is caused by the artificial tempo that has been created. As the artificial machine time we are forced to live by acts linear, forcing us into the rapids of the river of time, only giving us enough to react without thinking. Pushing us to the limits of what our internal roots can handle. A system that is meant for the destruction of our individual sovereignty — whether it be frequency, identity, or time — as if we are supposed to live our lives in a perpetual state of fast forward.

Until we hit the brakes in a moment of internal clarity. Stopping to take a deep breath of air, where all that fills the ears is the slow rhythmic thumping of our heart. With each deep breath the lungs expand and contract the chest to the biological rhythm of our bodies. To feel the compression and storage of our internal energy moving not horizontally, but vertically through ourselves.

In that moment of clarity, we simply become "we are." Claiming the vertical present, as now our energy moves up, just as the sap in a tree. Not horizontally, from before and after, giving our energy of time to the mechanics of the outrage matrix.

In one solid breath of clarity, a total focus happens in which our attention becomes a single-point singularity where our time sovereignty becomes more in depth in the time that we have in the present. As "I am." The total focus of our internal clarity that casts aside the mechanical vertical time energy of jitter of the 808-grid, deadlines of "getting it done," the anxiety and regret, while dissipating our energy of time. As we are no longer walking through time; we are living in the moment. Becoming biologically and chronologically efficient.

Living in a moment that the matrix refuses to allow us, as it continues to hijack our long-term mental drift. The algorithms that are run by the machine use short-form hijackings by lowering the formats of the videos we see on such places like TikTok. As the durations become shorter over time, lowering our attention spans from 15 seconds to 8 seconds — shorter than that of a goldfish. Removing the ability for us to reach the long-form drift.

Almost like a precision-guided frequency weapon. The aim is to give us a burst of dopamine, conditioning our brains to crave constant novelty through each swipe. Effectively leading to "brain rot" that weakens the prefrontal cortex, affecting our focus and judgment. Leading to slow, effortful tasks such as reading or deep work feeling physically painful.

Looking at the long-form drift, it does counter the 15-second life created by the matrix. As by focusing on activities that push past the 10-minute mark, we can reclaim the acoustic shield that the sovereign lineage of music provides us. Allowing us to live in the "present" deeper, leaving our brains to reconnect with the executive control network of the frontal parts of our brains. By retraining ourselves to focus on our internal selves, or focus on any project for a duration of 10 minutes, our sustained attention returns, overriding the craving for novelty.

Not only is it about the fracturing of time into seconds away from minutes caused by the algorithmic dictations of the internet. The "conveniences" of modern life play into the temporal fracturing. At one point in time, humans used to work for their livelihoods — not just with a job, but in other factions of life such as food preparation, household chores, finances, and almost every aspect of life. Where we had to go to a bank for financial business, cook our own food from scratch, even wash our clothes by hand.

Over the decades we have seen that all change for the price of convenience in our lives — aspects all designed to give us more time in life. Yet what now do we do with that extra time? Has our life actually improved? Or have we just added more activities to our lives to alleviate the boredom of having extra "time" on our hands?

Have the conveniences in life actually created a better life, or have those conveniences become a temporal parasite? As life becomes frictionless, our tolerance for effort declines, keeping us in a chronic state of sympathetic dominance. A place that we end up as we give up our evaluative authority to predictive systems. In a sense, we become a passive partner to the conveniences in life as we begin to skip the journey to end up at the final destination. Reaching a point where we become voluntarily dependent on the temporal parasite that is. Looking at the concept of dinner for many: most people order out, where a person orders, the food arrives, it is paid for, then eaten. Skipping out on the old-fashioned method of gathering the items, preparing them, cooking, then eating. Skipping out on the most fundamental part — the journey from the beginning to the end. Missing out on the life experiences and honing the skills of cooking. Just as it is the same as any other aspect of life when it comes to conveniences.

The friction, or the "hard way," essentially is the antidote to convenience. Or in another form, the antidote to cognitive decay. As we can look at the hard way as the journey in between where we become the sovereign director of what we are doing. A concept that can be seen as being in an intellectually stimulating environment — an activity that can physically reverse the aging of our brains.

Looking at it all, we don't lose our sovereignty in a single moment. We lose it through one convenience at a time.

There are one of two paths to take with regard to time. One path takes us down the artificial passage of time that leads to entropy. As the artificial time is linear, fragmented, and extractive through the 15-second clips of the internet, or the artificial urgency that comes from the unhealthy community. All to keep our minds in sympathetic overdrive, causing the temporal fragmentation. Or in other words, we may be alive for 50 years but we only own 10 minutes of the time as we have let the matrix pickpocket our own true currency. As we end up subscribed renters in the world as we biologically burn out.

The second path could be considered the fountain of youth, as with our biological time that leads to homeostasis within us. As with our biological time, it is governed by our circadian rhythms — our natural 24-hour clock that runs our biology of resting and activity. As well as our ultradian clock that runs on shorter cycles such as 1–2 hour cycles, cycling other aspects of our bodies such as our behaviour, psychological and hormonal actions within our bodies. Guiding the rate at which our bodies repair on the cellular level as well as the recovery rate of our own frequencies. Biological cycles that can be seen as another form of long-term drift.

As we decide on which path to take, it is up to each of us to determine the path. As one accelerates our lives through the horizontal deadlines and fast-paced frequencies, the other leads us to the slowing of the external friction within us; to a place that we start inhabiting our own biology. As we become masters of our own moments, not slaves to the artificial metronome in the silence that surrounds us.

Silence is one of the key elements in our own sovereignty, as it is a concept that reclaims our temporal grounds. Silence itself is not silence as in the absence of sound. Silence is the absence of the external noise around us. Looking at the previous arms of music or even in the external identity of communities, one of the main hooks is the constant "screaming" that causes crowding — temporally or acoustically — to keep our internal selves from ever becoming empty. So that we can never hear the biological hum that rests within. Just as some may call the hum the natural frequency of the earth.

Just as with the Schumann Resonance — a natural resonance that comes from a complex interaction of the earth, storms, lightning, surface, and atmosphere — creating a hum to the baseline frequency of 7.83 Hz. A hum that we cannot hear in the artificial noise of the matrix. Yet a hum that we can hear and feel within ourselves as we look internally in silence. That is where the reclamation of our sovereign time happens, using silence as a shield to manually override the noise of the matrix.

Our bodies, specifically the vagus nerve, retune themselves to the earth frequency, putting our bodies in that state of homeostasis. To repair ourselves as well as giving us our internal clarity — acting like a cognitive reserve to protect us from the storm surges of the matrix. That is where our unsubscription lies, as we don't need to do anything to become sovereign. We simply stop vibrating with the machine as we can now own the ground we stand on and the minutes to breathe.

As we can see now as one of the reasons for the three musical arms of our times: they were designed in mainly two specific ways beyond just harvesting our emotions — to either harvest our time or show us how to reclaim our time. Just as with the long, drawn-out riffs of the sovereign lineage arm. Songs that last 10 minutes or longer that are designed to let us become introspective, as well as showing us how to regain our sovereignty over time. To return us to our true timelines of our biological clocks.

Just as going through the physical and psychological stages of internet detox. To push ourselves to be or live in our internal and external silence by pushing us past 10 minutes. Breaking the 15-second spell of the algorithmic clock. We can now let ourselves sit for longer. Ten minutes work into one hour. One hour moves into one and a half hours. To the point that we have reached clarity within and without ourselves, rejecting the horizontal timelines of the ghosts of the past as well as the anxieties of the future. Anchoring us in the vertical present of now, where we now command time, not be managed by it. To live in a slow, unified, intentional time as compared to a fast, fragmented, reactive time.

As of now we can call ourselves the masters of our own time. We can now use time to our own advantage to push back against the unhealthy communities that demand our attention now. Just as the urgency that the matrix pushes on us. We can use our own biological clocks as a way to lag, by refusing the instant replies of the collective urgencies that un-synch us from the collective rented wars. Ultimately making us anchors where the collective persona must slow down to meet our frequencies. Where we maintain our own time and energy so that we can contribute to the healthy community when it actually matters.

Now we are "living on time" as compared to spending time. As time becomes a medium of existence — not as a currency to be liquidated through survival, distraction, or validation. A sovereign rhythm that protects not only us but our gardens in which we grow. We can live life in which we are not spending an hour; we are living an hour. An hour that the matrix can no longer steal from us, as we do not have to live in a reactive state where our biological energy is no longer spent on the demands of the outrage matrix, leaving us in entropy and exhaustion.

Instead, we are left in an active resonance. As we live in the vertical presence of now, vibrating as the minute. Not using the minute, as our internal clarity becomes so razor sharp that the idea of loss through reactivity vanishes.

As I sit like I have for the last three months, looking out the window to the sun rising in the morning, my sense of time has certainly changed, as the feeling of urgency has left just as the artificial time faded away into a memory. Now with my new morning routine of just sitting in the vertical present, I can feel the rhythm of my own biological clock ticking. I don't feel the need to be in a rush anymore, as time feels slower, as there are no more storms swirling about. Just a steady calmness of silence.

As with leaving the outrage matrix and rented wars of the digital world, time now feels as if I control it. Or I should say: I have a lot more time in the day. Time that I control in a sense that I can enter the long-form drift without feeling guilty of wasting time. By not filling every waking moment with the external noise of the matrix. Just sitting now thinking of nothing in particular — living and feeling the now.

In the beginning, it was just a few minutes here and there. Eventually drifting longer to the point that time just disappears, leaving me immersed in the natural environment around me. Almost like viewing life through a video that I can pause to look at the still picture, to see all the small nuances of life. The smaller things that would've been missed living to the fast, fragmented pace of the artificial time.

As with all, the day must go on. Like all, I must venture out into my own community to take care of my own duties in life. In which now I walk to my own biological time, set in the realm of the artificial time that many around me walk to. As now, it feels as though I walk between two timelines, as if I am seeing the world through the lens of a movie camera. Whereas my time is ruled by me, overriding the artificial time through the boundaries that my internal identity has created.

Chapter 8: Motion Sovereignty.

Monday morning — they are always a great day. A start of another week, another blank slate in life for us to strive the stories of our lives on. Some people, it seems, frown on Mondays as it is time to go back to work. Personally, I don't mind Mondays, as they are just there. Another reminder of time moving forward; not in a linear motion, but in a cyclical motion.

I must admit though, it is a rather loud morning, as it appears to be a snow-clearing morning. The community of public works crews are hurrying along, clearing the streets before the people wake up to be on their way. From what I can see in the morning light, there is a steady stream of dump trucks in a field not far away. Driving in, dumping their loads. Driving away just as fast, as their box gates slam back and forth. Not giving any time for the box to fully lower, creating a constant loud thud in the morning air. Just as the orange and yellow lights reflect off the houses into the window. As the grader speeds back and forth, scraping the roads clear, creating a massive windrow in the middle of the road — all for the big snow blower to fill the trucks and move on.

It is quite an orchestrated event to watch. All the equipment operators working in unison, yet all vastly unique. As each piece of equipment is different, but they are all out accomplishing the same goal. Just as a sovereign person acts within a healthy community. Like sovereignty in motion — a well-oiled machine of independent operators all working for the same cause. I am pretty sure though, that if I hopped on social media this morning, it would be filled with people complaining of the noise as early as 5:00 am. But then again, it would be the same people complaining that the roads are impassable. People and their external identities; they are never happy.

Personally, it is a minor inconvenience, as it is the last week of February — February 23, 2026, to be exact — where I am sure it will be the last inconvenience of this kind for the winter. As for checking social media to see those that complain; I think I will pass. As this past week marked my third month of abstinence from social media, I certainly don't see the need to break my abstinence for such trivial reasons in life. I have truly grown to accept my new path in life.

My challenge now is to sneak out of my own little spot in the world without becoming an inconvenience myself to the community clearing the streets. As I drive around the community that I live in, it is rather interesting the sights I see. Just like anyone in their own community, when a person just notices. Sometimes it's the bigger things, such as people working together on construction projects — off in their own worlds, building away. Or the people walking or biking down the streets. Some eternally glued to the screens of their digital devices, oblivious to the surroundings around them. Acting as if they are impervious to everything — walking out into the middle of the roads without looking. Expecting the world to watch for them, not watching out for the world themselves.

As per my usual routine, my drive takes me past the local gym. Always the blinds open, as people jog upon the treadmills. Some pointed outside the windows; others pointed to the walls in front of them. All jogging next to each other at their own pace, wearing headphones or earbuds. I had always wondered about the earpieces themselves. I do get the idea that they are meant to be a “do not disturb” message to the rest around, as most go to a gym to work out — not to socialize — or that music helps with the duration of an exercise routine.

It does feel though, that a person may be missing out by being plugged into headsets for the sole reason of being alone within a group. It is not so much the social interaction, but the noise coming through the headphones. Noise that cancels out our own natural noise, as our feet hit upon the treadmills as we jog along. Our hearts beating to the pace of our working bodies, as our breath becomes labored from the intensity of the workout. All drowned out by the external noise of ear sets — our natural biological rhythm that elicits our flow states.

As it is up to personal choice whether to listen to external noise or not, there is the possibility of tuning into our own natural beats — of our bodies. As with jogging and listening to our own mechanics of our bodies in action, that can take us away to our vertical time. To feel our bodies to the point we become lost within it, living in the depth of the present. Leaving our minds blank to start drawing its own picture on the wall in front of us — running outside in nature, where our mind feels natural to drift to — all the while jogging on an indoor treadmill. To the point our minds and bodies become fully enveloped in our internal worlds. Until the buzzer rings "stop," as now the flow state has been broken.

It is a state that many of us have been in — the flow state. Personally, I tend to live in it. Mainly by accident most times, as I get so involved in my activities that the rest of the world just melts away. Leaving behind all concepts of time, just immersed in what I am doing — living in the flow state. That is one of the great things about getting lost in an activity of any sort. Time just seems to disappear, where the external consciousness just disappears, to bring about silence. Just as after a long productive day, with wrapping up the evening chores. Retreating to a quiet place in the house away from the world. Drained of physical and mental energy, to just be. To just exist in the vertical time.

It is not a mechanic that is about being mindful, nor "living in the moment." Vertical time is a shift in how we use and experience time. Just as horizontal time is about the past and future, vertical time is the depth of the present. The erasure of the fragmented, linear, reactive, external tempo of the rest of the world. A state that collapses the past and future to enter the present through clarity, as our biological clock becomes the rhythm. As our attention becomes singular in total — not through a psychological process, but through a biological process. As one starts to unwind for the day, many processes start happening. Our breath starts to deepen as the anxiety fades away. The heart-rate variability becomes higher, as our nervous system shifts from the beta frequencies to the theta.

Stabilizing our internal rhythm from which our attention becomes unified. A state where the artificial urgency of the outrage matrix loses its grip as identity conflicts fade. A state where our internal clock takes hold, pulling us into a state of clarity that the matrix can't touch. As the outrage matrix thrives in the past and future, unable to touch us in the vertical present. Lighting the flames of our sovereign agency.

It is hard to say how many people understand how our lives are controlled by the external influences of the matrix. As we go about our lives, believing that we are in full control. Yet the power of the outrage matrix is a strong beast that truly does attempt to control us. Where our agency is one of the many shields that protect us from its hooks. As agency is not about taking control of our lives, confidence, or our motivation. It is when our internal tempo becomes stabilized that we choose to act in the direction that we want to go. To maintain our boundaries — to move without being pushed. This motion that is internally generated creates our agency.

Almost like an internal biological engine that starts with vertical time as the ignition, fueling our agency to set ourselves in motion. Creating a perpetual cycle, like that of the pistons in an engine moving up and down. From the vertical time of internal ignition, to the agency of the first motion after the ignition. Back to the vertical time of depth, to the agency of direction. Leading to the vertical time of coherence and the agency of action. Finally, to the vertical time of sovereignty of perception and the agency of sovereign movement. A self-directed movement within us, all created by our internal selves.

As with a treadmill, the matrix itself prefers us to live on the proverbial treadmill. In a sense of false propulsion, where we think we are moving, yet we are really not. Just as with the digital form of the matrix through its pings and notifications. Where the 15-second dopamine loops keep us in a chase mode for information and validations. To make us feel like we are moving forward, yet we are stuck spinning our wheels as there is no torque behind our actions. So that we can never push ourselves out of the matrix. As our sovereign motion requires high-energy intent to move. Just as in actually walking down a path from point A to B; we create a starting point to see the finish point. We push our bodies to start moving, all the while our senses are taking in the sights and sounds around us. Ultimately coming to the end.

As now our motions are architectural and weighted by our internal sovereignty, as it is our internal force that gives us the torque to move forward. As compared to the entropic movement the treadmill or the matrix gives us. As our steps become deliberate and weighted as we move forward. Creating the difference between "action" versus "activity." As action is the initial alarm, creating a high tempo of bitterness and anxiety. Creating friction within us that ultimately keeps us on a circular path that is the outrage matrix. Whereas activity is our internal vision and command, leading to linear structural gain through a calm and steady tempo. Or one could say, "grace under fire." Almost like a paradox, as our quiet internal selves are strongest when we move, as our frequencies are grounded. Creating the inertia to move forward. In a sense that the matrix cannot move the mountain of our internal sovereignty, yet it can trip our external identity as it runs.

A concept that had never crossed my mind was the constant jumping in and out of the outrage matrix. From my own internal sovereignty and agency. Or leaving the matrix to be in my sovereignty. Just like many others, we just do it as that is the way of life created. It may sound like nothing or that it does not affect us in any sort of way. However, a large amount of damage is done by skipping in and out all the time. Damage that could be viewed as deep-sea decompression. Leaving our coherent sovereignty to immediately jump back into the matrix's horizontal time. We are immediately flooded with the pings, notifications, and social media noise. Creating an information overload, pulling our minds out of the alpha and gamma frequencies of focus and creation. Slamming us straight into the high-beta frequencies of panic and reaction. Effectively draining our internal batteries of the energy we stored in the vertical time, as well as short-circuiting our batteries of the flow state we were in.

Sometimes it does feel like running headlong into a brick wall —going from vertical time, living in our sovereign agencies, to the horizontal time of the fragmented, reactive state of the outrage matrix. To prevent running headlong into the brick wall, it is about slowing down or creating an energy buffer in between. In terms of refusing the digital calls for 20 minutes after we leave the vertical time or flow state. To allow our ultradian cycles to finish off their cooling periods after our sovereign activities. As well as literally touching grass or naturally grounding to the earth. To feel the natural rhythms of the earth. In reality, it brings a whole new meaning to "don't go swimming 30 minutes after you eat."

The whole busyness of the world does feel as if it is based around the Pavlovian concept of triggering us with a noise to get a reaction out of us. Instead of ringing a bell causing an animal to drool while waiting for a snack, we have been conditioned to the sound of a digital notification to elicit a dopamine reaction. Or a reaction caused by the involuntary action of the external tension created by the notifications. An action that creates internal tension, where we move to join the arguments, buy the product, or just check the pings. We release that tension. Which is not our agency; it is the biomechanical harvesting of our internal energy. As our movement is caused by the signal. As compared to our sovereign motion that originates from our quiet self into our vertical time. A motion that is weighted by our own clarity, giving the forward motion that cannot be tripped by the external world. Creating structural change around us through the motion of the impulse that hits us. Standing strong against the impulse that pushes for a reaction—being of our own agency once again.

Our agency—more precisely, our biological agency—where we participate and maintain ourselves. Not through our will, but through our homeostatic protocols. Through our self-determination to shape our own ways through life. Through our developmental paths that respond to the alternation of the internal and external states. Maintaining our agencies through the predicted sensory feedback with the actual sensory feedback of our minds—the will of our intent on the backdrop of the true results of our actions. Leading to our agency finding a place between the stimulus around us and the response we give. A biological action of our prefrontal cortex overriding our reflexive action to give us voluntary command of our bodies.

A concept of how our minds work just as computers; a top-down system in which our brains use executive commands to handle the unique situations that lie outside our automatic psychological processes. Creating an inhibition control that overrides our automatic reactions, or our prepotent reactions to the external forces of the outrage matrix. (In a different term, I could go as far as saying "indifferent," or stoic to the external forces around us.) As agency is not a choice. It is the lock on our attention—the output of our energy. Where we can now look at agency as a biological function of the requirements of life, rather than the psychological function of our lives. As we can see, it does appear to come down to action versus reaction. As our internal sovereignty moves to build and construct our worlds through our own biological timelines. Just as the outrage matrix itself relies on our reaction to fuel it and to drain us. As we do not move to our internal rhythm, we react to its signals. Just as moving from a chair—do we move from the chair on our own agency of just wanting to get up? Or are we moving from the chair because an external influence has made us? Creating the working environment of our gardens or the mechanical will of the matrix?

As with the physics of the world, kinetic energy is a fundamental component, just as within us. Kinetic energy pushes us forward, utilizing the resources within us—energy. Just as time sovereignty, we have resource sovereignty within us. The ability to govern the natural wealth of our internal and external selves. As with the outrage matrix that treats our resources as Liquidation units; such as our biological energy and attention. The outrage matrix utilizes a resource-dependency strategy to maintain its external hold over us. Using such things as "convenience" for our primary needs, we centralize our resource management to artificially high levels so as to never charge our sovereign batteries. Creating a power imbalance in which we forget about performing activities "the hard way," as we have surrendered our sovereign rights over our own gardens.

As our gardens are our ecosystems. An ecosystem that is about the right to own, control, and use what is for the well-being of our internal selves. Not the external world, as we can define our own environments around us. In terms of what to be and how to feel away from the noise of the matrix. Creating a circular root for the energy that we create. Just as with a healthy grove of trees—communicating together yet being distinct. Using the same soil and water, yet only taking what they need. Weathering the storms as well as reshaping the environments around them. Not through just reacting to the storms and environments, but by breaking the winds to reshape the world around them. Just as the passion of the fires of life flows through the trees, creating their own agency.

As it is not about the matrix wanting to actually kill our will; it wants to automate our wills. That is one of the greatest tools it has against us. Just as in the pacification and activation arms of music, the whole idea is to outsource our evaluative authority to predictive algorithms. So that our biological agency is replaced by a reflective loop. In which, through predictive personalization, we end up in the mechanical will. As the matrix steers our choices of the "recommended for you" and rewards platforms, the machine ensures we pick the path of least resistance in life. A default path that leads to our own executive control becoming dormant, to the point that we are no longer willing in life. We are just living a recommended script—we think we are making decisions, yet all we are doing is matching the matrix algorithms.

That is why we must always choose the harder paths in life, no matter how uncomfortable they make us feel. To take back control over our internal sovereignty, as it shocks our prefrontal cortex back into command mode. As now we have put aside the conveniences of life, or the path of least resistance. To make ourselves think for ourselves, to create the kinetic drive to motivate us. To expand beyond the external environment around us. Our drive in the world by taking a moment to think about what we are doing or seeing. Just as being placed in a dangerous work situation that could turn a mundane task into a potentially fatal situation. Taking a minute to stop and breathe, creating a sense of lag in our presence before we move forward to react. Or to deliberately move at our own sovereign pace, relying on our own resource sovereignty through applying intentional friction to our motions.

Intentional friction—the process of adding extra steps to our motion—re-engages our biological will of our internal territory through our active agency of deliberately challenging ourselves. Creating an air gap that stops the mechanical will of the matrix, which uses reactive optimization of passive compliance from the external algorithms. A subscription model that is applied to our souls. Whereas our biological will overrides the mechanical will, giving us back control over our agencies.

The control over our agency is what the world is all about. Or the lack of control over our agency, to fall into a state of compliance with the system. A system that is being designed to have total control over all resources available to us. In a sense, it can be viewed as a global artificial accountant—a system designed to count where all units of energy are being stored and used. To maximize the efficiency of the harvests of not only food and energy, but our own bio mechanical energy. One of the biggest challenges that is faced is the resource sovereignty of our own physical movements through the artificial tempo of the world.

Just as with the musical arms, as well as the concept of the community persona or identity, frequency entrainment is the most effective weapon the machine has against us. As the main trap is moving at the artificial speed of responding to the instant demand of the outrage matrix. Such as walking and staring at our digital devices, biking, and checking in traffic. Just dropping our worlds for the instant high-frequency reactions. A system designed to leak our sovereign energy in a way that merges our nervous system with the matrix. That is where air-gapping the reactive state of the mechanical will with a time lag is key. As we can now "ghost" the system and live in our own sovereign state. As the temporal air gap becomes the beginning of the untracked journey, where the algorithms cannot lock onto us if we refuse to synchronize ourselves with the noise of the system. Allowing us sovereign action that removes the psychological aspect from the equation, realizing that our actions are a high-energy working event, as opposed to reacting to the external environment.

Which brings us back to our gardens—our sovereign gardens that can now be seen as a vector of every action we make. Actions that now hold both magnitude and direction of our will, which leads to a self-defined direction. Or a focal point. Without a focal point, we are just following a random, high-entropy movement of the matrix. Allowing us to become the lead operator in our external worlds as we move the world; the world does not move us. As with a focal point, we become a fixed point where the outrage matrix dissolves around us. Just as a vector, the idea is to become so internally heavy—just like the internal roots of the tree—We become unmovable to the noise of the outrage matrix. As now we choose when and how we move through the matrix, invisibly, just as ghosts.

Other than completely unsubscribing from the rented wars and outrage matrix, walking as a ghost is the next best step. As we can see the external world, yet it cannot see us. Now we can return to the great coliseum of chaos not as participants, but as sovereign observers. As we re-enter the coliseum, our silence of being em-pathetically, passionately indifferent gives us the "armor" needed to resist the noise of the coliseum. With deep grounded roots giving us the weight to not be caught up in the storms. As well as our own biological time that allows us to create a shield against the reactive nature of the outrage matrix. We can now move freely about, although the eyes of the coliseum are always watching through the algorithms.

As with the world itself, it has become heavily regulated by "monitoring" our every move. From the algorithms of the internet to the surveillance cameras that watch us. Even with the purchases we make, the travels we make—almost every aspect of our lives is now monitored. All to extract value out of us, as well as to keep us compliant. In reality, I could go as far as to say that humans are being pushed into a new state in the future. A state that is unfolding before us, moving us towards a governance run by artificial intelligence. It may sound like some strange science-fiction fairy tale, but the signs are all around us. Many countries have already adopted this state, with many more to follow to reach a specific goal by a specific date.

It is not hard to see that everything is being monitored. We monitor our heart rates via smart devices; we are monitored in traffic, at the grocery store, and by all the smart devices around us. Everything on the internet monitors our presence, which is common knowledge. The way we walk, our bio-metrics, our movement patterns—all monitored as the commodities we are. As we have now reached a point where bio-metric identity frameworks are continuously used for invisible authentication across all public and private spaces. As the matrix uses real-time location systems to track equipment and resource flow, including us. Just as within the coliseum—the eyes of the machine are always watching us. Even if we do not see those eyes, our walking movement is being measured without our consent, creating an identity linkage across both the digital and physical worlds.

As we walk through the coliseum, or past such eyes, as strange as it sounds, the true way is to walk abnormally compared to how a human would walk—confusing the eyes upon us. Just as with the internet itself. Some say that VPNs and staying anonymous is the proper way to go, or that keeping one's behavior erratic confuses the eyes that watch us. It is something we must know as we walk about. For it is our kinetic signature that is scanned, linking us to our metadata. Walking like those who are subscribed to the rented wars allows the matrix to map out sovereign gardens well before we can even build our fences. The objective is not to hide from the eyes per se, as in being stealthy like a ghost. It is to resonate at a frequency that the matrix cannot own. If our own tempos are sovereign, we are seen as background noise. In a different principle, people often say that the best way to go offline is to completely delete all apps that keep a person tuned in. The idea is sound; however, the algorithms keep scraping our information, finding ways to pull us back in. After deletion, we lose control over how our personal information is used. It may be deleted from our screens, but all the information is still stored away on a server that can be accessed at any time in the future. To be used as a reference to put out a software patch to hook a person back in.

To navigate as a ghost in the machine, the obvious thing is to have very limited information to begin with, all the while using social media to post the abstract and mundane things in life. To blend into the background noise, to be seen as irrelevant, as compared to drawing the machine's attention. It is a process that I see all too clearly on a regular basis. I do have to check emails; by doing so, I am now always bombarded with emails directly from Facebook telling me what I am missing, who is saying what, or who is posting. How many notifications I have missed, etc., all because I just abandoned my Facebook account. I never deleted it; I have just ignored it. However, it is proof that the matrix is watching our behaviors and patterns, doing what it can to hook us back in. The whole idea of being at stealth is to not leave an afterglow or a digital shadow by stopping continuous authentication, as well as wiping the table when we are done—deleting all local data caches. Or after a high-attention move, randomizing the temporal delays so that we can return to our internal sovereignty. Leaving no digital tail behind us. As now the eyes cannot steer what they cannot see, as our internal intent stays private. As it is not about being successful by moving fast; it is about being successful through being discreet.

It is a rented motion that has been installed upon us, as we have been essentially possessed by the matrix. Our bodies do not belong to us, but to the machine itself. As we are being pushed into a chemically reactive urgency designed to keep us running on the proverbial treadmill of being busy, yet stationary in our vertical axis—creating entropy that bleeds out our sovereign energy. To collapse the rented motion, to reclaim the biological momentum, once again we must stop and refuse the push signal of the external forces. To find our quiet self in a feeling of heaviness; collapsing the rented motion of lightness. Restoring our sovereign motion by our own internal commands, leading to the sovereign navigation of the coliseum around us—we march to our own rhythmic drumbeat.

As we stand to walk through the bleachers of the coliseum, we can now go from being tracked by the eyes around us to intentionally moving by our own internal triangulation, held down by the bio-mechanical anchors. The anchors that ground and synchronize us to the natural frequencies of the earth. Where if our vagus nerve feels jittery, our navigation has been compromised. We use our internal compass to not navigate where we want to be in the horizontal time, but what needs to be done in the vertical time. All the while knowing that our biological symmetry is the only anchor that can be used to navigate through the coliseum without succumbing to the noise—the non-reactive silence of our internal sovereignty.

As we walk around the Coliseum, there are two paths ahead at this point. One can be identified as the script of the matrix. As before, one path is the pre-approved path of convenience. The other is that of high-energy friction. This is where the air-gapped lag of a lead foot comes into play to identify which path is which. As the scripted path is always filled with the speed of ease and optimization, leading to a highly tracked path by the eyes around. As it ends up in the horizontal time of validation, creating an entropic dependency. Whereas the true path is filled with resiliency through the vertical time of our internal commands, leading us to not be seen by the eyes around us. Ultimately, taking us to a place of autonomy through our integrity and depth. To where we can truly construct our internal gardens. Giving us the right to move through the coliseum not as a public data point, but as a private, sovereign being. A being who can now move through the world, as our subscriptions have been cancelled.

Moving not because the world is screaming around us but moving because our gardens require construction.

Chapter 9: Navigation.

Another Monday of opening the window curtains to see Mother Nature burying the world in yet more snow. It is as if she doesn't want to release this part of the world from the icy grips of winter. On the bright side, the calendar has turned another page to become March 2026. In the desolate wastelands of winter, there is some optimism to be had. As the adage goes, "March comes in like a lion and out like a lamb." Or vice versa. Maybe spring is around the corner, as it is hard to guess Mother Nature's plans. I must admit, depression does start creeping in a little bit—the desire to feel the warmth of the sun, the fresh new greenery again. A change from the constant whites and greys of winter. It is always a time to look forward to, even if it is living in the horizontal time a little bit.

Meanwhile, to pass the time, I believe vertical time is the place to be, given the high-frequency pulses the outrage matrix has been putting out. It is always the usual noise—a geopolitical event happening someplace or another. An event that grabs the world's attention by the ears, permeating into the lives of almost everyone. Except for me and the ones who read this. I know what is going on; I have just elected to stay out of it all. In all honesty, some of the events that are happening today in the world—I was given fair warning years ago. Now the theater is playing out to the masses who subscribed to the shows.

As my own days pass along, I have contemplated many times about starting my digital detox at a different time of year. Perhaps I should have started in the spring when there are more outside activities to keep me occupied, instead of the dead of winter when the hooks of the outrage matrix are the sharpest. But then again, I would not be where I am today—far, far away from the noise. Or is it just a bad habit of doing things the hard way? These are just questions I ask myself from time to time, with an answer that always comes back: I am not missing anything. Nothing at all. In fact, I have gained more than I lost—my internal sovereignty.

But alas, it is time to move. At least this morning it is not about dodging snow-clearing equipment; instead, it is dodging road construction. It is rather odd to see such construction at this time of year, but there it is—hampering the daily commute for many as the main road is blocked. I'm sure it is an inconvenience many of us have experienced in our daily commutes, on the routes that we become entrained to take—a daily driving routine that is almost always a set path. The same route day in, day out, rarely breaking from the path. Although there are many different paths to take through the maze of civilization, it is always the most comfortable one we choose.

As I drive around past the intersections, a reoccurring thought always crosses my mind—the decision to go in one direction or another. To turn left or right, to take a different path, or to continue straight—the most direct route. As with life itself, every decision we make can change the outcome of our future at every intersection of life we come to. It is a thought worth considering some days.

Personally, I do not rely on the modern conveniences of "GPS" or an artificial voice telling me which way to go. I have relied on a rather primitive method: the memories of exploring different avenues and streets. To go down different intersections when I choose. Even to the extent of relying on the direction of the sun and the moon, as I follow archaic directions of "turn left at this distance" or "turn right." Running on a hope and a prayer, I reach the final destination down a labyrinth of backroads. It is not the fact that I don't trust modern technology to guide me on my travels. It is an internal compass that directs me—a photographic memory of sorts. I usually just need to travel to a destination once, and my mind has the route physically registered in my head—a physical mind-compass, per se.

Looking at it, one could say that we have a few compasses within us. Or a compass that operates on different layers. Just as I can say that I have an internal compass that guides me in my travels down physical roads, I can also say that there is a compass that guides my internal self as well—just as everyone has. We all do have the bio-mechanical setups within us; it just comes down to how well-used our mechanical setups are. Just as an internal compass, or as others may say, a moral compass. Or simply our internal compasses.

The problem with a compass is not knowing we have one; it is how to calibrate it to our "true north." Without the proper calibration, we are just on the high seas of life. As with the artificial tempo of the world that creates an acoustical and digital wind to push us off course. Our internal biological states point us toward our true north. As with the noise of urgency, conflict, and even propaganda that hits us as we navigate, it tries to trigger our sympathetic nervous system—to disorient us by pulling us into the outrage matrix.

To stay on course with the true north of ourselves, once again the temporal lag is the mechanism to keep our internal selves stabilized under social engagement pressure. Even just one long exhale of our lungs is enough to create the temporal lag to stop the noise from translating into stress—putting the brakes on our vagus nervous system as well as our heart rates, keeping our internal clocks from synchronizing with the pace of the noise. In a sense, pulling our attention back to the physical world around us. All the while focusing on the weight of our bodies through our feet and hands—a proprioceptive awareness. Or grounding ourselves through our own weight to the earth. Or stepping back with our eyes to view not only the high-frequency noise, but to view the whole environment around us from a distance. To allow us to see through the noise, to realize the noise is not a threat at all. It is just noise.

As with orienting our internal compasses to the noise, the tone of our compasses holds great value in our ability to navigate the waters of the external world around us. Just as with the tones of the musical arms that use frequencies to bypass our senses and affect our nervous systems. When our nervous systems resonate on a high tone, it lets us see the enhanced pattern-recognition loops around us—where the urgencies and emergencies can be seen as repetitive cycles.

Just as the basic foundations of the rented wars and the outrage matrix themselves. The noise only moves us if we resonate with it. Yet, if we resonate at our own baseline frequencies, the noise just passes through us, and we continue to move forward unfazed as a non-resonant entity in this world.

It is all a deliberate desynchronization by the outrage matrix, as it sends out a “pulse” to us in the form of urgency—all to keep us in a state of reactivity. As the world demands our immediate attention through endless loops of urgency. However, by keeping our internal frequencies dialed into the natural resonance of the world around us, we can mimic the external appearance of the artificial tempo that has been set—keeping our internal momentum decoupled from the urgency of the crowds around us by pulsing with the crowds to remain invisible. When we separate ourselves from the artificial tempo, we can stop and change directions instantly, as compared to being bound to the momentum of the system. All set by our own biological clocks.

As when we maintain our internal clocks, we can take the signal of the pulse and transform that signal into background noise. Or white noise, allowing us to move through the noise—not vibrating to the frequency of the signal. All to maintain our direction through the external signals via inertial navigation. As we can rely on our internal gyroscopes by defining the direction in which we can proceed. Such as basic needs like food and water. Biological cycles of our bodies, as well as core objectives in life. Where we filter the pulse of the urgencies and treat them as background radiation against our fixed reference points of life. So as to become non-resonant, as the frequency of the crowds does not pull us off course, as we become too heavy or anchored in our internal root system to be moved—just as a fog rolling through. The fog may obscure our view, but it cannot move or change our paths.

As before, the way we interact with the external forces is more of a bio-mechanical structure compared to a psychological one. Detecting the external pulse is a visceral contraction within our physical bodies. As the artificial tempo hooks onto us, a shift in breath occurs as it moves from the deep diaphragm to the upper chest—giving a feeling of tightness as our bodies prepare for the sympathetic flight response. As the matrix convinces us that there is an urgent and immediate threat pulling us off course until we stop to take a deep breath down into our diaphragms.

Depending on the strength of the external pulse, our ears and eyes are affected as well. As we fall out of our internal rhythm, foveal vision begins—our eyes become narrow-focused, with our hearing tuning into high-frequency sounds that we perceive as threats. Finding that we are fixated on anything external, whether it be a bill, a screen, or a problem. A state where we lose all peripheral awareness, becoming focused on the predator that lurks on the edges of our internal lights. With the ever-growing feeling of knots or a fluttering sensation in our stomachs, as our bodies shut down the rest-and-digest state to divert our blood to our limbs—all setting the stage for our physical fight or flight. Whereas if the gut feeling does not relax, the matrix has tuned into the internal frequencies of ourselves.

Just as before, expanding our vision away from the focal point of the pulse—outwards to see every corner of the environment around us—is one of the ways to counteract the pulses of the outrage matrix. Just as taking the time to diagnose our breathing to see if it is shallow or deep. To feel for a clenched or relaxed jaw. To feel our heartbeats—whether they are in a steady hum or a frantic pulse. To biologically feel if we are living in our internal sovereign selves, or hijacked by the external, urgent pulses of the matrix.

As we have not left the great Coliseum of chaos from the previous chapter, where we are simply walking around avoiding the eyes, it is imperative to understand the symptoms of being poisoned and corrupted by the matrix. It is a biological safeguard we do have within us. If any of these safeguards are compromised, it is time to step back to the garden—to recalibrate and rest.

To switch topics for a minute, throughout this chapter the vagus nerve has been mentioned. A part of the human anatomy that I feel compelled to speak of before moving on. The vagus nerves, from what I understand, are the second-biggest nerves in our bodies—one running down the left side, one down the right. Extending from the medulla oblongata, down our necks, and into our vital organs such as the heart, lungs, digestive tract, etc. The vagus nerve is part of the parasympathetic nervous system that regulates our major organs in terms of heart rate, rest, digestion, as well as our fight-or-flight response.

It can be seen as the main nerve that controls our homeostatic state and the overall well-being of our bodies. There are many different ways to consciously regulate our vagus nerves through sounds and vibrations of our mouths, as the nerve does pass through the back of our throats. Although, it is up to the individual whether they believe such practices work. The underlying factor is that the vagus nerve is part of our involuntary nervous system that acts like a two-way highway between our brains and organs—the part of our bodies that reacts to the external forces of the world through our internal organs. So, as our chest tightens to the external influences of the world and our hearts speed up from the urgencies of the pulses of the matrix, our vagus nerve reacts internally.

It is a point worth noting, as people think that the external influences of the world create a psychological effect within us. The case can be made that it is a bio-mechanical effect that creates the tension and emotion within us. The psychological aspect can be seen as a side effect of our bio-mechanical interaction with the external world—or in other words, a scapegoat to blame our internal/external friction on something. As it seems that humans always need a scapegoat when our identities become snagged.

Identity snag is one of the surgical strikes the outrage matrix uses against us to have us subscribe to the rented wars. As it focuses on our egos when they are leaky—like an improperly functioning valve that the matrix exploits. If we do not take the time to repair the leaky valve of our egos, our internal sovereignty is siphoned off, pulling us down into a defensive, reactive state.

Isn't that what the digital and social world is all about? How to play on our egos to elicit a reaction from us? As with the matrix itself, as it knows through predictive algorithms what makes us feel right, relevant, or respected. In a way that presents a contradiction that threatens our reputation—our knowledge being challenged. Or placing us in a category that we feel insulted by, such as unintelligent, ignorant, or unskilled. Pulling us physically as we feel the need to defend our identities. As well as feeling the need to demand justice and correction when we feel that we have been wronged. Where we can spend hours arguing with others to correct what we believe is an injustice to ourselves, when it could be a simple mistake. Resulting in trading our silence and internal tempo for the satisfaction of being right. All the while not realizing that we are letting the matrix win, as it has successfully paced us. All the while our vagus nerve locks as our heart rates spike as they synchronize with the artificial tempo—putting us in a position where we are not defending our lives; we are just defending a data point. All to be recognized as being "right."

That recognition demanded by our egos leads to the validation loop that the outrage matrix thrives on—a validation loop that uses the hooks of a "verified" badge, or being a part of a gold tier. Giving the feeling that a person is "in the know" in the world, as if their information is only known to them and no one else. Essentially adjusting the interval vector to maintain a "status." Whereas a person starts acting not in a sovereign state, but because they look sovereign. As that is what is being expressed—just as with the digital gurus who say that by following them, a person will gain insider knowledge of the world. When in fact, they are just looking for the subscription payment. All the while leading us to become predictable so that we become quantifiable and steerable by the rented wars. Ultimately leading to our subscriptions to the outrage matrix.

As much as the matrix hooks us using frequencies to overdrive our nervous system, it hooks us through our ego and emotions. With the best defenses being that of taming our egos, or dissolving them completely. It is a concept that sounds easier said than done—the removal of the ego. As it is the system that always seeks validation and recognition, even when we are not seeking those attributes consciously. Interacting with others is when our egos rise to the top, or in our interactions in the digital world as we hide behind a screen, becoming fearless. Where everyone is wrong and we are always right, to the point where the main attack is another's ego. I am sure we have all been in a position where our "egos" are to blame in our beliefs, opinions, or values in life. In which the term "egoistical" comes into play as a way to pacify one in an argument—all in the name of winning.

At some point, we have to step back from our egos to see the world for what it is. A rude person in our daily lives, a slow system that creates a temporal inconvenience—even people on the internet of different ideological beliefs. To see that we are all generic players wearing a mask. When something happens to us in life, it is the mask that it is happening to—not our internal or external selves. Where we have to step back, take a breath, and realize it is a system error. Not a soul-shattering event; not something to care about the matrix understanding. But to be passionately indifferent.

There have been many times that I have let my own ego get the best of me as I traveled down the paths of life. To come to a point where I was wrong in my decisions, where I find myself looking inward to my own internal roots. To realize that I made a mistake and that it is time to correct my path. To stop and reorient myself and continue the course. I am sure it is a common experience in the human experience of life. In a way, we believe that we can never be wrong—a true sign that a person leans heavily on their external scaffolding for support. For myself, I have learned that to err is to be human, as it is a natural part of our evolution. If we did not make mistakes, many positive evolutionary advancements would never have happened. So, it is my belief that we are meant to fail so that we know how to succeed.

Many will disagree with my last comment. Unfortunately, it is something that I see all the time. I am sure many of you do as well—the failure to admit being wrong. To stop, reorient, recalibrate, and move forward. It seems that some people will hold on to their beliefs for as long as they can, defending them to the death. A feature that the matrix thrives on—almost like the foundation of it. With the digital world being the most prevalent of this attitude, to the point that some become so immersed that it becomes their world. All because of the time spent looking into a topic—years of their lives invested. Bringing about the most tragic ironies: people can spend years dedicating their lives to an ideology or belief, to the extent that they will leave their own blood—their true tribe—to join the tribe of others, defending their beliefs to the "death."

On the other hand, people will cultivate relationships or marriages over years and decades—if not lifetimes—only to push them aside because of irreconcilable differences. I'm not sure, but that has always tugged on a couple of my internal roots. That people have no problem moving on from relationships over matters that can be resolved, yet will fight to the death over an ideology or belief that has little influence over their internal lives. I don't know. I would sooner admit that I am wrong—something I do all the time—correct my course, and move on. I find that my integrity is more valuable to me than being right in a conversation, even when I know I am wrong. All to save face in the eyes of my ego.

Now to get back on the path that we are walking—through the great chaos coliseum of the outrage matrix. With all the noise circling us, from the social media warriors fighting for whatever cause to the storms that swirl above, we do have protections to keep us from being sucked back in—to keep us from becoming subscribed to the rented wars. Through the grounding of our internal agencies in our roots, to be temporally delayed so as not to react. To walk in silence, impervious to the highly reactive state around us. A state that keeps us from inheriting the pace of the frantic urgency by keeping our own internal pace through our delayed actions. Of stopping for a breath of air to prevent our heart rates from being entrained to the frantic energy.

Where now we can view the chaos that surrounds us from a wider angle—from our peripheral vision—as compared to focusing through tunnel vision. As to not feel the speed of the fast-paced world around us, grounding ourselves with the weight of our internal roots. To feel the weight of our feet upon the ground, creating a heaviness that consciously anchors us from the pull of the abstract stress of the storms above.

Walking with intent, or a slow wave, against the high-frequency noise. Resonating to our own frequencies, as we are no longer part of the artificial world's resonant frequency.

As with the noise of the coliseum, we can detect the frequency of the noise through our internal orientation of our true north. Leading us to identify the source of our drag from the environment around us—to scan our external worlds and see the hot zones. To become so heavy that we can see the biometric mesh of the matrix, so as to pick the path of least resonance. Leading to a state of "check" with our internal orientation—to be autonomous from the external environment. So as not to become a target of the urgencies.

Just as the day goes by, bringing on the dawn of the evening, it is time for one more course correction—to begin the walk out of the coliseum back to our own gardens. Just as in the real world, as it is time to check out of the office for the day. To reverse our morning commute to return home, as staying in the coliseum for too long becomes a fruitless endeavor. Just as staying on a course that leads to a dead end, or realizing it is time for a change. It is time to recalibrate ourselves through the physical detachment from the artificial tempo, for when our nervous systems start to become agitated with the feeling of urgency. It is now time to move away from the stress of the outrage matrix, as the terms of agreement have never been negotiable—we can snap back to our gardens at any time.

As we snap back to our gardens, it is one last commute home for this entity—to finish the work week for the weekend. To have time away from the external pressures of the world—to recharge and live in my own garden. It is a disconnect commuting back home, as I adopted the habit ages ago. As with my commute, I leave the external world behind so as not to bring the urgencies and pressures along with me. They can stay where they are. Far from my home and my garden, as there is no space for those forces there. Home is the ultimate shield from the outrage matrix itself, as it is like a vampire—it will only come into a residence if we allow it. If we don't allow it, it will sit outside in the environment doing no harm to us.

It is the same concept, I find—leaving the lands of the outrage matrix and rented wars—the commute to and from the world past my home. For when I put the key in the front door, my world awaits. Opening the door to walk inside, shutting the external world behind me as I close the door. Removing my footwear with a deep breath, feeling the decompression of the day behind me. Standing in minutes of silence as I look around and realize I am home. Back in my own garden, where now any external force created by the artificial world is up to me to ignore—which I have come to do in the greatest of ways. For the artificial world can now wait for the convenience of my own internal biological clock to respond—if it decides to respond at all. As now everything external is behind me. Just as the fading sun on the horizon signals the end of the day. As it is hours before it is time to turn in, the curfew time of 7:00 pm. has hit. The time to put all digital devices away, with the sounds of urgency hidden even more. To let the rest of the circadian rhythm play out as the moon rises in the sky.

Chapter 10: Boundaries.

I do see today is the biannual event- the day when the clocks spring forward. The only real grace is that it falls on a weekend, sometime during the night between Saturday and Sunday. The only way I would really know the date of it, if I didn't look at a calendar, would be from the very few digital devices I own. The ones that get the automatic updates. The rest of my time devices- I must manually change the time. As for now, I live in a temporal limbo. Stuck between the digital and analog time. One hour ahead, one hour behind until I get the intent to change them all.

There is no better way to fragment our circadian rhythms by such an abrupt change, as now our sleep has shifted one hour. Meanwhile, nature and the animals that live within it have stayed in their natural times. As with my own animals that live under my care-supper time is still supper time to them. They don't care about a time change as they know when it is feeding time.

From the human aspect; I did enjoy seeing the rising sun in the morning. Now I must wait another month to experience that ritual again, although there is more light in the evening. To enjoy the evening sun after work now, giving a slower pace than frantically getting activities done before the night. Personally, I find the time change as a minor inconvenience in life. For I know that I run on my own internal clock, more than the artificial clock of the world. As I wake up and fall asleep to my own time- only running on the artificial clock when I am moving through the external world.

It does show though, that the external time is artificial as it can be changed so easily. It is a worry that I won't have to deal with until the morning, as today is Sunday. A day not to worry about such details. I do know one thing though, when I arrive at the office in the morning. There will be people complaining about the time shift. As well as many other "urgencies" that have descended on the world, as it appears the outrage matrix is in a high pulse mode these days. All over the rising costs of living due to certain geopolitical events happening halfway around the world. An old conflict that was started by one party to create "change" that did not have the desired effect. Which was just "managed" for decades, to the present where the party that instigated "change" on another. Is now trying to "correct" the problem, to be seen as heroes. Or something like that. To me, if certain global parties just stayed in their own lanes. We would not have the conflicts we see today.

I suppose though. The machine needs to feast, so a rented war it is. With that, I do believe I know what the subjects of conversations will be for quite some time. Unpleasant topics that threaten the way of life for many; the rise of the cost of living. As that is a direct threat to all, it will be hard to escape such conversations. For it may be one of the greater hooks to have us or keep us subscribed to the rented wars.

Personally, as for what I have been doing over the last four and a half months. I have been largely ignoring the 24/7 news cycle as it is nothing new. For during my time in the outrage matrix; the groundwork of what we are witnessing today. Was laid out years ago- the rest of the world is just catching up.

As much as I hate to say it, getting away from the rented wars is quite difficult. As being unsubscribed to it all, the ghost pulses still hit every once in a while. Just sudden little bursts here and there- a reminder from the matrix. I could not put my finger on why I was experiencing the ghost pulses; just a quick flicker of an external noise as I sit far away in my own garden. It was when I realized that the ghost pulses were not coming from me. They were coming from the others around me- the ones that are fully subscribed to the rented wars.

It can only be described as a biological residue of the artificial tempo- the ghost pulse. As our nervous system picks up on the environmental frequencies around us. With our vagus nerve being 80% sensory, it may be tuning in to the stress response from others around us. Leading to second hand stress from the collective anxiety of others. Given that our Vagus nerves run our fight or flight responses, it is always scanning our environments for threats and emergencies. For when the people around us are locked into the fight or flight state created by the urgency of the world. Our sensory system locks into the tones and pitches of others voices. As well as the facial expressions of others, to determine a threat.

Just as with the concept of "herd mentality."- one gets spooked, the rest of the herd is spooked. Just as our own systems mirror the states of others around us. The ghost pulse that may hit us from time to time, may not be from our direct involvement in our external worlds. But from involuntary involvement from the ones around us.

To help counteract such pulses, setting up a perimeter of control of our boundaries is an effective solution. As much as we think that boundaries are designed to keep people out, they are about protecting our internal environment. As it is the limit of our tempo, silence and identity. Not as a static wall itself but the limits of where those states can be breached.

In one aspect, we can view boundaries as a working or kinetic perimeter. In terms of the concept of the 6-foot radius around us. A physical boundary that puts physical distance between us and others. (I am sure we have all heard of this concept before. Mainly during the great pandemic of the early 2020s. As one of the main protocols was to keep a 6-foot perimeter around us, as to not catch a virus.) Ironically, the same air gap measure falls into our boundaries between our external and internal worlds as well. Just as the Vagus nerve is our sensory to the external world, it is extremely sensitive as well. With the close proximity to others, our Vagus nerve picks up the secondhand stress stronger. As by having physical distance, it lowers the secondhand stress frequencies from others. So as the crowds around us rushes in urgency, our physical distance allows us to breathe within their stress field entraining our hearts.

Even as we function within our residences, we do create an insulating threshold from the world. Where the perimeter of our properties defines where the matrix's leverage ends and our own sovereignty begins- we no longer are a customer. We are the lead authors on our own comfort. Just as with the digital perimeters as well. We must view the digital perimeter as data Compartmentalization; by understanding that the digital world is a tool to be used as a disposable interface. As the internet is a tool to be used, not us being the tool being used by the digital world. As what we do in the digital world, stays in the digital world. As it has no need in our insulated boundaries in a way that our pulse that we put out in the external world does not follow us back to our internal selves. By creating a perimeter that the internet can look for us, but only find our shadows.

Our boundaries not only protect our physical worlds, they are a multi layered defense system designed to filter out the external chaos. As to keep our internal tempos anchored to our natural frequencies. Allowing us to keep our own intent, instead of having our nervous systems fall into a constant vigilance. Reacting to every social and digital pulse around us. With clear boundaries, it allows us to hold a calm state when we reach deep focus. Or engaging socially with others. As our ventral vagus complex can apply the brakes to our heart rates. All the while regulating our neuroception of the environment around us. Where we are subconsciously scanning for safety, preventing us from being triggered by the artificial urgencies. Putting us in a position that we have temporal insulation from the always on world we live in. Giving us the ability to dictate our own internal pace so as to reclaim time for our gardens. Not only do our boundaries protect our silence and identify. It protects our tempos through the circadian alignment of not engaging in high frequency noises and pulse. By setting up curfews for ourselves, away from the digital pace as well as the rented wars. (It is a routine that I have always been fond of. Shutting all digital devices off well before bedtime. As to not have the day's event stuck in my head for sleep time.) a natural decompression from the day.

In the modern day of all things convenient. Once again, it is about doing things the hard way. It is not only good for the growth or our internal roots and identity. It is also good for the boundaries that are established as well. One good example is paying our bills in society, such as utility bills- a monthly ritual that we all perform. On one hand, we have the super easy convenience of digitally paying our bills. Just got a couple of buttons and the bill is paid for. On the other hand, there is the manual payment of bills by going to an actual brick and mortar building. Such as a bank- my preferred method as the people know me by face. Not through showing identification, but through the nod of a head and gentle salutations- like two sovereign people identifying themselves through a hand less handshake.

Going through life manually does make life a little harder as now a schedule has to be made to allow the time to get to the physical locations. As per the quick ease of the digital world, yet. Without the digital world of convenience; we would be living in an analog world anyways. By living by a more manual approach, we remove the algorithmic predictability of the matrix. An approach that creates a barrier of time and mass. While the utility bill is being paid in person physically, the light speed on which the matrix works at, is forced to now work at the speed of our physical selves. Putting the matrix in a position that it now cannot predict or download our intents or patterns as we communicate through physical objects. All the while protecting our identities and tempos through the laws of physics, not the laws of algorithms. Just as the deep growth of our internal roots. Our boundaries allow us to say "no" at any time, even without saying “no.” As our boundaries keeps us from being pushed off our natural frequencies. Allowing us to become deep rooted to move.

Even when we sense that our physical or kinetic boundaries are being breached. We can perform an emergency drift sort to speak. Just as with the physical paying of utility bills, we end up around others in this world- some people mind their own business. Others tend to let the world know they are there; the ones that tend to get a little aggressive for no real particular reason. Perhaps a threatened external scaffolding? Or the impatient ones that think that they can speed things up by standing in the 6 foot boundary zone, trying to elicit a high frequency response from the people around. Usually leading to a pulse of high frequency exchanges of words and actions. That is where the emergency drift comes into play, as one direction is to go Gray by de-escalating our voices and facial expressions. Giving the other person a low-resolution version of ourselves just like a mask. Putting our egos and righteousness aside, to allow the pulse to wash over us. Provide no resistance for the outrage to grab onto- drifting in a zero-friction state until the interference passes.

No matter if it is the bio mechanical, digital, or physical drift. The concept is all the same, as when a boundary is breached by sensory or frequencies. Hacked and compromised as in the digital world. Or an event occurs one must leave their homes, seeking refuge elsewhere. It is about staying in a non-reactive state, moving along to the next place. All the while disconnecting when a breach occurs. To let the outrage pulse think it has won, all the while staying to our natural frequencies and tempos. To move on in life. Or as I like to say, to be indifferent or stoic to the storms that blow through. Storms that are of no soul shattering importance in our internal worlds.

Detecting our boundary breaches is about monitoring the signal to noise ratio of our own biology. As the matrix breaks in through frequency contamination, where our internal frequency is interrupted by a pulse that is external. Such as the case of the digital world where an event happens, and we are left thinking about it later. Leading us to be standing in our own insulated homes, wondering why or how an event has happened. Or staying up late into the night with an overthinking mind, trying to decipher the day's events. That is where our tempo boundaries have been breached, as the internet has successfully occupied our mental real estate. Leading to a course correction of immediately unplugging from the external world to find the silence of our gardens. Through tasks that bring us to our flow states.

On a bio mechanical level, it is the same concept of the herd mentality of which I experienced. We are around others that are in a state of high urgency or stress. So our own nervous systems naturally pick up on the states of others, to mirror the reactive state of others around. A point where we should hit a dead stop in all forms of movement; to take deep breaths and planting our feet firmly on the ground. To counteract the shallow breaths and jaw clenching that comes from the mirrored stress of others.

Even with our identities themselves, it is always the snagging of our egos that cause a boundary breach. Once again, through the need of feeling right or understood. Where we feel an injustice has been done to us, as we start to feel the need to become indignant or defensive over an error.

Snagging our egos by a hook as we formulate a logical argument in our minds, or preparing for battle- however one wants to view it. All the while successfully tuning our ego into the pulsations of the matrix's frequency. At that point, we must remind ourselves that "As a sovereign individual, there is no need to fight or argue with the machine." It is where our generic masks come into effect, to allow us to drift through the issue. So that we can vanish back into the shadows.

As much as we have to look at the external forces breaching our boundaries. We must look at the internal forces as well. These are the silent leaks of energy that tricks our systems by dropping our biological brakes, giving control back to the matrix itself. One being the obvious; urgency.

Urgency is the mainstay of the world; it is our deadlines, our instant responses, and the fast-paced nature of the world. As well as the state that pushes our nervous system into the fight or flight state. It is the temporal acid that breaks down our internal tempo, as to let it become hijacked by the outrage matrix. Leading to our subscriptions to the rented wars. Without the artificial urgencies created, we would all live in silence amongst our gardens. As I had mentioned before, it is all about time itself. Or time sensitive demands being made to us, where we abandon our internal rhythms and tempos to mirror the matrix's frequency. Putting us in a state that we no longer move with intent. We begin to move in panic; pacing ourselves with the machine. All the while feeling a sense of guilt if we do not subscribe to other's actions.

Guilt is another identity snag that is often internalized. I am sure we have all felt guilty at some point in life, where we are called to participate in an event of some sort. An event that could be associated with the pacification or activation arms.

Or with the collective persona. An emotion that can feel like a tug inside of us for not participating or fulfilling a role others expect us to. Leading the matrix to use our own egos against us for its own expectations. Guilt does create internal friction as it slows our sovereign motion by hesitation when we become worried about our own optics in the non-sovereign world. Leading us to hesitate on performing a drift or a hard disconnect from the external pulses. Or in another term, a guilt trip to convince us to act or react when it goes against our internal roots. A hook to become subscribed to another's rented war, as when the guilt trip does not work. High frequency responses follow, such as insults and non-compliance to the collective persona. Leading us to feel obligated when we do not need to be.

The concept of obligation is in a sense, the cornerstone of the terms of subscriptions to the rented wars. With any interaction in the external world, we end up "owing" something or another to another entity. We owe to our utility company, which is fine as it is a reciprocal trade- money for heat and shelter. The basic necessities in life that we work for as we are obliged to hold up our end of the deal.

On a different level, our obligation is treated like a number on a ledger as in an unhealthy collective community. Where we must adapt to the collective persona at the expense of our internal identity. Leading us to feel obligated that we owe the collective something- mainly the ultimate currency. Our time, where we are pushed to feel obligated to subscribe to the collective persona's rented wars nearly by being in the vicinity of the unhealthy community. Our own labor at our jobs is another example as well. We view our labor as an agreement for time to be paid in a fiat currency. All the while being pushed to be obligated to work longer hours. To take on heavier workloads, to meet unrealistic deadlines. All the while eroding our own metabolic perimeter as we let the pulses of work bleed into our insulated homes. All the while bleeding into our silence.

At this point, we must view urgency, guilt, and obligation as synthetic signals in order to stop the erosion of our internal boundaries. As urgency is just a hallucination of our clocks and a personification of the artificial, external clock. Where guilt is just a ghost in the database, meant to haunt us when we perform our sovereign actions. With obligation just being a contract for the matrix- a way to unwittingly subscribe us to the rented wars. Meanwhile, our internal agencies and insulated homes that we live in. They don't care about our guilt or the urgency, as they simply are.

Now that we see the corrosive nature of those three aspects, we can shield ourselves by refusing to resonate with the distress caused. It is not ignoring the world; it is refusing to participate by filtering the external signals coming our way. But by shielding our nervous system through our voices. For when we are approached in a high frequency fashion that creates a tightness in our throats or a spike in the pitch of our voices. We can now turn around to respond in a lower pitched, slower vocal. forcing our vocal cords into a low frequency, relaxed vibration. Sending a safety signal through our vagus nerve to remove the urgency. Leading us to feel no urgency when our throats are vibrating in a calm sovereign frequency.

Just as previously described, the matrix hooks our identity through the tunnel vision it creates inside of us. Through the outrage we see, or the bill we stare at intently. To allow our sympathetic system to take over just as with the prey focusing on the surrounding environment for any dangers of predators that may be lurking. The matrix is designed with the same intent- to keep us laser focused on dangers that are not there. In which to counter the tunnel vision, we must step back to view the whole room through our peripheral vision. Inhibiting our Amygdala to a state that now it sees more than just a threat. It can now see the whole room around. Realizing that the threat is only a small fraction of the overall picture we see. As now, we refuse to let the noise occupy 100% of our field or view.

In a whole different context and scale. We can apply our vision to a global scale, to where we can move to a satellite view of the earth. Or a 40,000 ft view; to be able to zoom out of the smaller external pulses that we view as tunnel vision through a microscope. To view the whole world as a whole- being able to zoom in and out as we please. Realizing that the external pulses that we see under the microscope that look huge and significant. Are actually smaller pulses in a world that actually has relatively few pulses that are designed to illicit a reaction out of us or erode our boundaries.

As with the metabolic boundary- a boundary that focuses on our metabolism. Or in a different term, how we expend our biological energy. Whether it be through the high frequency paced outrage matrix. Or storing our energy in a parasympathetic state.

It is all about how we manage our daily energy. Leading us to the metabolic shield as obligation and guilt could be seen as corrosive enzymes. Enzymes that thrive in our shallow chest breaths as we react to the external pulses. Whereas the diaphragm can be seen as our internal pump. Hence, the importance of stopping to take deep breaths that enter our gut region. To entirely focus on a long drawn-out exhale. As long as possible, to push out the enzymes by putting the brakes on our Vagus nerve. Slowing our heart rates no matter how guilty the matrix tries to make us feel. Allowing us to stay good with our bodies, as the report of our nervous system is coming back as being in a stable condition. No matter how loud the outrage matrix is reporting a crisis. Allowing us to filter all external pulses through our biological gates, keeping us out of both fight and flight states.

When the word boundary is mentioned. To some, it assumes the meaning of withdrawing or isolating oneself from the world. It is a likely assumption, as that is how the word is presented by some groups. In terms of our internal sovereignty, boundaries are not walls around us, such as the prison walls of the outrage matrix. Boundaries are lenses that we use to bring our true vectors into focus. Whereas isolation is the state of disconnection and in some cases; entrapment. Our sovereign boundaries are a state of selective connection, by hardening the perimeters of our boundaries. We are not cutting ourselves off from the outside world; we are clearing the signal to noise ratio so that we can see the world for what it is.

With no boundaries for our internal sovereignty, the world becomes a blur of priority pulses created by the instant urgency we are faced with. By enforcing our boundaries, we are filtering out the high frequency flicker of the matrix. Leading to a clarity where our harder manual paths become high definition in our lives. As we no longer need to guess what to do next in life, our natural frequencies dictates the next move. In reality, becoming the difference between reactivity and panic. As compared to being calm and stoic.

In our own identities, our sovereign boundaries do not create isolation that leads to loneliness. It leads us to become distinct from the rest of the world, as we are shielding both our internal and external identities. To which the labels that the matrix creates for us no longer stick to our souls. Leaving absolute clarity on who we are, because we are not trying to be understood by the matrix anymore. Not only does our sovereign boundaries create an absolute clarity. It brings about deeper relationships with others, as they are built on bio-verification that are shared frequently. As compared to digital profiles.

Leading us back to the chaos coliseum itself, with the swirling storms above. As we can now clearly see the matrix for what it is as, by not spinning around in the storm itself. But by standing still in the storm as it rushes around us. Letting us view the matrix for what it is; a visible utility. Not an all encompassing reality.

Now, here we stand with our internal roots firmly planted in the soil of our gardens. No matter how strong a storm blows through, we have zero shift as our clarity is absolute. Where the noise of the storm has no mass behind it to move the trunks of our trees. As our boundaries do not isolate us but liberate us to what is real. We just are.

Chapter 11: Authorship.

Another day. I would have to say that the curse of the temporal shift is slowly slipping away. As much as a person prepares for it, the time change always wreaks havoc on the circadian rhythm. Eventually, it will all settle down. Synchronizing once again to the natural rhythm of life. At the very least, it is halfway through the week- Wednesday, March 11, 2026. With only a couple more days until the weekly routine wraps up, leading to a well deserved break from the external world we all live in.

But alas, soon it is time to get myself motivated for another day at the office. As it is not quite the end of the week yet. Nor is it time to leave yet, as I sit enjoying my morning routine of sitting staring out the window. Listening to the morning silence. It is quite the change from waking up to proceed with endless scrolling to find out what I missed in the world, as I slept. For the world never stops, does it? It just keeps spinning around, just as the events of the world. Churning out new stories- new hooks to keep the world subscribed to the rented wars.

My routine is pretty basic; I wake up an hour and a half earlier from when I like to be at work. Waking up to the morning routine that I feel comfortable with. To leave at a respectable time, to be half an hour early to work. As to adjust to the coming events of the day at my own time. As to come a custom to the new day on my own accord- to move to my own tempo.

As the morning moves along, the rest show up on their own time. Usually showing up just before the buzzer rings to start the shift. Where most sleep in; to frantic rush to work; to start working. A concept I have never understood- to start the day to the sound of a shot gun. To hear the alarm go off. To get ready and be out the door, with no actual time to adjust to the day. Almost like starting the day in a reactive state right from the moment their eyeballs open. To continue through the whole day in that reactive state to the end of the day. Repeating the same schedule for weeks on end- to only look at the weekend as a moment of reprieve.

Over the course of my career, I have met many people that perform in the same fashion- frantically rushing to be someplace on time. On my end, I enjoy the sovereign progression. Starting the day on my own tempo through my own intentional movements. Taking the time to check my own nervous system; to make sure I am calm and collective. To be able to see through the external forces with my discerning eye.

Discernment is the weapon or defense that we must wield in this world. Not only to strengthen our boundaries against the external pulses of the outrage matrix. But to guide our internal sovereignty. As it is the flickering flame that guides us in the dark, as well as the catalyst of our moral compass. Giving us the ability to determine what is right or wrong- to understand the difference between the truth and falsehoods. Opening up our minds to become wiser, insightful, and introspective. It is like the two flickering flames that burn within us. Allowing us to become sovereign over our own motions, as compared to reacting to the external environment around us. Leaving us to write our own stories in life, just as an author writing a book. Lost in the written words, penning away with no heed to the world around.

Just with an author writing a book, our sovereign lives are a biological example. As with every movement we make, thought and tempo shift are an act of our original intent. Allowing us to navigate the world through our own itineraries- not a world built by others. Giving us the absolute responsibility of our sovereign selves. Removing the urgencies and obligations of the matrix, as we become our own poets of our lives.

Is that not one of the many meanings of life? To write our own scripts, while acting to it as well. Realizing that movement is an internal revelation, not reactions from the external stimuli? Moving to the cause of the experience; not the cause of circumstance? To move not because the system demands us to move, but to move because we have decided to. Where it is our will to move, not because we are being pulled. Realizing that the matrix and the algorithms of the digital world do not run our thoughts. We cultivate our own thoughts, just as we cultivate our gardens.

Now we become the own authors of our stories, as we turned off our antennas to the external pulses of the matrix. Instead, we become the broadcasters. Whereas in the non-sovereign world, people become echoes or reflections of the external pulses and pings. As now, we produce the pulses and pings. For we have the internal mechanisms of our own nervous systems to pace our breathing, to slow our heart rates. Instead of waiting for the world to calm us down, which it never does. It only wants us to move faster; urgently. As slow and methodical are the antithesis of the outrage matrix. Now we can perform our nervous system resets before we enter environments that are of high friction frequencies. Environments that now have to adapt to us- not us adapting to them.

Through our internal signal generation, we now move to our own wills, not by a trigger. Just as with urgencies that are pushed on us, we can pause to allow our internal signal to tell us when to proceed. Breaking the spell of urgency over us, as another's urgency does not translate to ours. Even with the idea of paying bills manually at a bank. We take away the autonomous nature, giving the manual control of life back to us. So that we move on our time, not the machine's time.

When one stops to think about it. It does feel that a lot of the external pulses are written by someone. Almost like a command sent out to get a reaction out of people, in one form or another. As though it is the terms of agreements unwittingly signed, when subscribing to the rented wars. An agreement that we have no obligation to follow. For our original thoughts are governed by our own comforts of silence, tempo and identity is the source of our own decisions. Nothing else, as it is our introspective commands of our bio-mechanics of our nervous system to halt all motions when we feel the matrix is screaming at us. Or when our internal signals feel dissonant in our gut. Shifting us from being a subscriber to the owner of our duration on this planet. Giving us the ability to perform the first move; the disconnection from external pulses.

Not only disconnecting from the external pulses of the world, by returning us to our natural internal frequencies. In which we can do a calibration of our internal frequencies by simply stopping by applying our parasympathetic brakes.

To slow down our nervous systems, to stop the over-reactions created by the machine. Allowing us to become the source of our calm. To feel the flames gently burn within us; the calm soothing feeling of a white flame that flickers inside. It is the same as our insulated homes as well, as we make sure we have the resources to survive. To be comfortable, where we can see the redundancies that we have created to know that there is no urgency. As we have self-authored the creation of our own homes- to be comfortable. All the while, decoupling from the artificial tempo of the ghost pulse, as we move when the time is right. Giving us a zero point to not only start our day, but to end it. As now, we have not only another kinetic shield against the external pulses. We have a casual shield.

The casual shield- a shield that allows us to have zero shift in the world. Just as the mountain as the fogs of noise drift past it. A shield that protects our internal signal generation where we can perceive the noise; it does not influence our points of origin. By not allowing our vibrational frequencies to match the external pulses and demands. We can see the information, to discern it as a disposable system. Keeping our nervous system in a sovereign state when we are hit by the urgencies of the matrix. Allowing us to mentally guard our source that identifies every move we make. Giving us the ability to stop and think, “was my movement my original intent? Or am I being pulled by a pulse? A phantom pulse?” If it is reactive momentum that makes us move. It is time to pull a temporal lag- to stop for a couple seconds. To recalibrate ourselves to our internal frequencies. Through indifference, we can decouple ourselves from the urgent external pulses. Leading to our manual paths in life, to have zero emotional investment in any external pulses. With being indifferent, there are no terms of agreements to the subscriptions of the rented wars. As our comforts are self-generated, leaving the matrix with no hooks to grab us. Leaving us with the ultimate shield against guilt and obligation- the outrage matrix did not give us comfort. So it cannot take our comfort away from us. Our emotions cannot be authored by anyone except us, no matter how hard the matrix tries.

In a world that is truly scripted by the news cycles, algorithms and corporate urgencies that produce the survival drama. Or the consumer comedies we see today. All based off of our guilt, obligation, or reactive urgency. Almost as if a ghost writer is writing a plot of constant scarcity and dependency to keep us all occupied. We can replace the narrative with our own script, as we are the authors of our lives. Through our precision and autonomy, we can now execute our own mandates in our motions. To see ourselves as a moving piece on the board, all the while. Maintaining our internal frequencies. Even with looking at our own insulated homes. We can see the physical evidence or our own authorship. As our homes are created for our own comforts, driven by our own sovereign motions. All the while, the rest of the world lives in anxiety. We live in a zero-shift environment where we live in a different book as compared to those that live in the outrage matrix.

Through our internal calibration of our nervous systems, as well as taking the harder manual route in life. We become the origin point of our motion. As we don't need to be a character in the ghost writer's script. We can now tune into our original voice- the frequency that remains when the noise of the matrix, or the noise of the great chaos coliseum is stripped away. Where we can now hear internal selves.

That is the one of the problems with the modern-day world- the concept that most people parrot what they hear. To just quote others or the ghost writer, as most just repeat the narrative of the machine. Leading to no original thoughts on events; just reactively. Or to just forward the script, as that is what is to be expected. Almost like the digital version of chain mail. Where we have to once again, stop to ground ourselves to our own nervous systems. To determine if motion is original, or we are just parroting the noise around us- whether we are being pulled into a high stress frequency or not.

Once we see the words that the outrage matrix uses to issue commands. Such as being "stressed" over a high frequency topic. We can refuse the script being offered, by forming our own vocabulary around the high frequency event. In a way that we can view an event not as a soul shattering experience, but as an experience that does not affect our internal sovereignty. Whereas we can discern an event from a mechanical lens, to understand that there is no existential crisis to our worlds. It is just a script of urgency created by others. All the while, allowing us to author our own experiences.

Even as the world turns in a high frequency state of artificial chaos. It is our silence that speaks the loudest, by allowing us the right to refusal of the pulsating panic. Whereas the tribes in the world panic and fight. We can sit in stillness; listening without mirroring the reaction of others. To not fall into the script's expectations of the reactionary worries. Leaving us to use our silence to incinerate the drama of the matrix, through our black flames. To reveal our own true thoughts and intentions, creating a coherent system between our external actions and our internal rhythm.

The friction in our coherence, between our external actions and internal rhythms. I am sure many have experienced this event in life. An internal drag that creates friction, feeling as though we are just being pushed through the world. Not flowing through the world in which we authored. In a feeling that our hearts are calm, yet our hands are rushing. Creating an incoherent balance within us. Whereby slowing our hands down to match the pace of our breaths. We can align our kinetic motion with our silence, giving way to weightlessness. As we are no longer interacting with the external forces; we are simply moving through. Just as with our homes as well, in the comforts that we live in that provide a coherency through the realizations of the redundancies we create- to have back up plans. Not out of the fear that something may go wrong, but to match our state of minds. Knowing that if anything may go wrong, we are prepared.

Through our coherence of our external actions and our internal rhythm. We can look at one of the bigger paradoxes that we face- our jobs. An agreement where we give our own currencies for the world's currency. All the while, operating in a high stress frequency environment. Yet, by viewing our jobs as a resource extraction point. We can stop seeing our jobs as time taken away from us, to see our jobs as energy harvested for us. Leading us to be able to remove the workplace friction allowing us to see total clarity as our internal purposes and external tasks are aligned. All the while leading us away from the herd mentality.

Our internal and external coherence does lead to the end of the struggle of the friction between our internal frequencies and external actions. As we end up outside of the matrix, whereby our pen ship. We are now just walking through the chapters we wrote when our day started. Now giving us the ability to move when we want to, forcing the matrix to adapt to our frequencies.

Even when a high stress event does happen, we no longer need to panic. As we can now drift through the event, allowing our internal momentum to slide us through. To not reach a state of reactivity by becoming nonresistant as the collective persona reaches a breaking point. Instead of holding our ground to become resistive, we perform the gray state maneuver. Of stopping to reset our voices; to stop and just nod or give a generic answer. Instead of attuning to the frequency of others around, letting the crisis just slide off our barriers. As there is no ego to hook on to.

Just the same as an event in our insulated homes, with say a utility going down. We simply pivot to our redundancies where the event does not become a survival drama. It simply becomes a recalibration of our systems, where we can switch from plan "A" to plan "B." All the while, keeping our tempo and silence. As we have authored the redundancies in our homes, to always offer us comfort.

This put us in a greater position as well, in terms of the greater geopolitical events of the outrage matrix. As now by authoring our own lives, we can change the script at any time.

Just as it feels like a ghost writer is writing the script of the world, seeing as it is a poorly written script of perpetual doom and gloom. We can just drift into the shadow and focus on our internal roots; refusing the panic of the outrage matrix. To ghost the emergency, as we are no longer characters in the script- leaving us to be hidden from the matrix.

By ghosting the outrage matrix and those who live in it. It is not about living in isolation. It is about clarity and focusing through the noise, to pick up the signal of other sovereign people out there. As much as we may feel alone in this world of high frequency chaos. There are many other like-minded individuals as well. All that we are doing is bypassing the social engagement noise, looking to connect with others on the same internal frequencies. With the digital world itself; it can copy almost every aspect of us. Yet it cannot copy our tonal sovereignty. As with the gray face approach, using low frequency speech and a soft gaze.

A person can determine if a person is affected by the outrage matrix's panic pulse of high frequency acoustics. Or if the person mirrors the silence and tempo. Allowing us to discern if the person we talk to is sovereign or not- to engage or walk away.

The way we communicate with others moves beyond whether another is operating on the same internal frequencies. As it is rather common knowledge that certain platforms do have algorithms that "listen" in on conversations. That results in the themes of the conversations being used to promote "for you" content on said platforms. By semantically bypassing the keywords we can become invisibly coherent to the algorithms, to make it seem as though we are just background noise. Instead of using the keywords that are used to track us.

Speaking in the language of our comforts and redundancies, bypasses such a problem. As the talk about the weather, cultivation, or the basics of work is just seen as small talk to the algorithms. Yet between sovereign entities, it can be a status report on life, in a sense. Creating a manual intelligence report- a concept that is quite effective. I have had many people under the influence of the outrage matrix attack me for using small talk. As for many, small talk is a waste of time. Taking away from the battles of the rented wars, leading to some rather nasty insults being thrown my way. Where people found it insulting that I would waste their time with talks of the weather and such. In my mind, being indifferent allowed me to drift through such attacks- it was all just water on a duck's back.

Just as meeting with sovereign entities living on the same natural frequencies. It is not about gathering to talk about current events, such as the pulses of the news. It is about being attuned with the natural frequencies of the others around. Leading to a strengthened group as a whole, as the friction of the news cannot infiltrate a group that has no one externally pulsing. Effectively creating a biological faraday cage with the people around. All the while, allowing us to be unsubscribed to the rented wars, while never losing our human connections and networks.

Looking back at the earlier spell that is cast upon many of the world- the biannual time change. Personally, I can say that I created a buffer zone against it. Whereas I have a routine of waking earlier than the ones that wake to a "shotgun" start to a day. It feels that I have aligned myself with my own circadian rhythm, as my day is not just about the 9-5 machine clock that many live by. It is about my whole day that encompasses all of my life in the day, allowing me to author my own temporal duration. Now by being able to author our duration. We can stop using the only currency we have to spend on a system meant to extract every second from us. Looking at our sovereign time that works in a cyclical, resonant, and biological fashion. We can align ourselves with high kinetic tasks with our circadian peaks throughout the day, creating an internal tempo that insulates us when the matrix demands urgency from us. In a sense, an internal metronome that paces us through the day. Ultimately removing the flat, linear, accelerating timeline dictated by the digital pacing and high frequency jitter of the external world. It allows us not to speed up to match the tempo of the matrix. It forces the matrix to wait for us, as we are the origin point of our own tempos. Allowing us to change the tempo of the seasons at our own will.

Looking at the external world through the subjective lens of discernment. The world does try and pull everything into peak productivity in one fashion or another. Leading to every day feeling identical, just as the proverbial rat race of society. Forever trapped in the concept of "Groundhog Day." Leaving the seasons to be either in the heat of summer productivity, or the winter of a systemic shock. Such as the shocks of the endless geopolitical events of the world. It is where we can look at our own metabolic seasonality; aligning our kinetic energy with our insulated homes. Learning that we don't need to struggle against the artificial seasons. We adapt and authorize them, in a way that when the world panics to a so-called soul shattering event. We can look to our homes; a place where we slow our pulses. To enter a deep freeze of silence and stillness, allowing us to conserve the potential energy we store. Not only physically but mentally in a way that the silence that we author.

Keeps us from being hijacked by the outrage matrix- to be drawn into the subscriptions of the rented wars.

Looking at the world from a bird's perspective, or a 40,000ft view. There is always a factor that creates panic and urgency that ripples across the lands- the rising cost of living. Or inflation; a narrative that certainly fires up the outrage matrix. Leading to a panic pulse across the globe. As the pulse ripples, leading to high stress frequencies and urgency. We apply the brakes to our internal clocks, before the external tempos reach critical mass in acceleration. As with the herd mentality, being in proximity to others in a state of high stress frequencies, our bodies will naturally try to match the same frequencies. In order to drift through such moments, through the intentional slowing of our internal clocks. We move physically slow to half speed of those around us. Instead of running with the herd, it is to slow to a walk. As to let the herd pass by- giving pause to any sentence that is said in a rapid conversation moment. Slowing our eyes and breath, as to drift out of the high frequency entrainment field creates. All the while, our internal tempo remains unhooked from the crisis while it sweeps over us.

Continuing on with the inflation theme, or the sudden urgency in say. The rising prices of fuel. It is common knowledge that through the herd mentality, humans tend to react by hoarding goods; rushing to fulfill a "more movement", as to cover the costs of goods. All the while exacerbating the problem. While the world mobilizes in a panic to hoard goods before they become scarce. (An event that I wholeheartedly see as ironic. For the whole event of mass hoarding only makes the problem worse.) A different path is to do the opposite of the herd- as little as possible. Retreating back to our insulated homes, with the redundancies we have created for our comforts. So as to reduce the need to hustle out of urgency, to see the event as a seasonal stall. To treat the crisis as a winter event, by slowing our spending and driving. Even our digital pulse. Ultimately increasing our survival duration, as well. Not to become burned out by the fuel of our own anxiety.

With the digital world itself, with the headlines of doom and gloom. As if time is running out with the end of the world near. We just kill the artificial 24-hour clock of the world, by authorizing a new duration. Reminding ourselves that the world does not run off the artificial time of the outrage matrix. The world runs off its own geological time of seasons, seasons that will not end for a very long time. Not from the news cycle time. Allowing us to temporally ghost the artificial clock- to move when our internal clock tells us when to move. Not when an "emergency" pings. An "emergency" that has no authority over our internal rhythms.

As with all "big events" that happen in the external world. They are meant to pull people, so as they can be towed by them. Dragging them along, to keep them subscribed for maximum harvesting. Be it through emotional stress, spending, or just by conversation. As to have autonomy over ourselves, it is our choice of vector based on our internal authorship, even when the herd is running in the opposite direction. As with the mountain surrounded by fog. The weight of the mountain stands too big for the fog to move it, as we anchor ourselves in our internal truths. The one we keep not as comforts in our insulated houses, but in our roots as well. By keeping ourselves resistant to the inertial pull of the herd, we can keep ourselves tuned to our natural frequencies. We can continue living our lives, as the event doesn't lead to the physical disruption of our home comforts. All the while leaving us on our natural vectors, not turning for a headline.

Realizing that we do have directional autonomy over paths, we can move how we choose. As autonomy is not about avoiding the matrix, it is about utilizing it for our own terms. Just as taking the manual hard way to pay utility bills- we move because we authored the move. A move to secure our basic human needs. All the while maintaining the gray man appearance, while our internal signal moves in a different direction. Refusing the reactionary drift of guilt and obligation to steer us, so our identities can decouple from the demands of validations and the labels provided. To move at our own tempo that we designed, as to not sprint with the world. But to maintain our zero shift- to recognize the urgency as a temporal hallucination.

It is where we, the authors of our own directional autonomy to refuse to be hooked by the sudden "catastrophic" pluses that hit the rest. By not resisting the pulse, but by drifting through it. To maintain our internal frequencies. Even when the pulse hits a manic pace, with all lost in a frenzy of anxiety and urgency. That is the time to decouple the ego, to give the most minimal response as not to cause a reaction with others. To not argue with urgency, but to just let it pass. Just as with the digital world itself, it is all based off of a poorly written script of a ghost writer. Where all we have to do is not read it. To drift back into our internal world.

I must add when talking about drifting. It is about yielding to overcome. To let the matrix think its pulse has elicited a reaction out of us. But in reality, we just moved ourselves to a different location. For we are the authors of ourselves, not the matrix.

At this point, we can finally see ourselves as the true authors of our own worlds. Just as we tend and cultivate our gardens, we learn to shape the conditions of our inner lives with intention. The external forces of the world may continue to pulse around us, but they no longer dictate our direction. Sovereignty becomes the act of guarding our time, nurturing our internal roots, and generating our own signals as we filter out the noise of the outrage matrix. Through discernment, we learn to recognize the frequencies that matter and release the ones that do not. And in moving with this sovereign clarity, we discover that we can slow not only our internal systems, but time itself—shifting the pace of our lives back into our own hands.

Chapter 12: The Sovereign Loop.

Monday morning, another week passed with a new week ready to unfold in front of me. As the page turns. Another empty canvas awaits to paint my own future, as there is no prewritten script to my life. At least I don't think so? Unless there is truly a Divine power that guides our lives- like an internal flame that lights our way? Or are we truly the authors of our own destinies in this world? It is only thoughts that cross my mind every once in a while- just the small questions that there really isn't an answer for.

But alas, it is time to head to the office to trade my own currency for currency that pays for my comforts in life. I don't necessarily need to work for a comfortable existence, as there are other ways to pay for life. One example is not working at all; to rely on handouts from the government if one so chooses. However, what fun would that be? Sure, I would not be trading my own currency for the comforts of my insulated home, yet those comforts would be severely diminished.

Or I could just ghost the whole grid and live off of it. Dedicating all of my currency of time to maintain the comforts of my insulated home. Although at that point, all of my time would be devoted towards that cause. To find a balance in terms of how I spend my currency and how I create my currency of time. I guess I would not be far off to say that I see my job as an anchor in my life. A place that I do not just spend time at, I create time- acting as an anchor in the world. A place that never changes, as the world changes around it.

As per my job, it is a rather unorthodox one. As the only real stipulation to it is to complete a full day and that is it. There is no actual structure of timelines or deadlines. No weekly quotas or expectations of workloads. There is no actual schedule to the productivity of work. It is just showing up to a clean slate every day to author the day. To move at my own rhythm and tempo- to create my time through my own sovereign motions. With no real distractions, except for the odd casual small talk. As well as the reminder that it is time for the customary mandated break period. Breaking the flow state that I find myself in, as I become so focused on my projects that time just slips away.

The flow state. It is quite the concept where our activities lead us to a mental state where time becomes fluid. Where we become so focused in our activities, that the external world around feels like it disappears. Leading to a perpetual cycle of thought and motion, just as with the sovereign loop that lies within us. A self-reinforcing loop that drives us forwards in life.

The flow state is similar to the vertical time, as they both take us away from the horizontal, linear time of the artificial world. Yet they are in opposition to each other. As the vertical time is living in the deeply rooted presence through stillness and silence. The flow state is achieved through being totally absorbed in an activity, where time becomes cyclical. As time starts to bend and compress, as it feels like hours become minutes. Due to our motion and attention merge, through identifying the outcome of the task at hand. Even before we start a task.

It starts through our optics of having the ability to see the outcome of a task. Before the task is even completed. Whereas identifying stops being a passive observation; it becomes the act of shaping and forming the outcome that we desire. Almost like a stencil or a mold in which our attention is poured through. Before we even start a task, we identify the geometry of the blueprint we desire to create. As once we identify the shape of our tasks. Our attention flows into the mold we have created, leaving the motion of time to pass by. Allowing the mold to solidify into our realities. Without being able to identify the end results of our tasks, our attention stays as raw unfiltered energy. As our attentions can work twofold. Just as with the focus of our attention, we can dictate the state of how our tasks are fulfilled- if we identify our tasks as chaotic. Our attention becomes chaotic. When we identify our tasks as a sovereign task, our attention shapes itself into a tool of precision. Allowing us not to just look at things, we can now render them by naming them.

As we focus our attention after we have identified the task. With ourselves becoming mobile in our activities. Our attention does not become a space to fill; it begins to warp our time that we create. As time is not a clock itself, it is a fluid state that changes viscosity with the intensity of our focus. A viscosity that can compress with our intense, unwavering focus. With our attention being focused, to the point that we are synchronized with our internal frequency. The notion of just passing time vanishes, allowing us to go through the perpetual state of the present. Creating a loop leading to the start of our tasks and end as the same energy. All the while our attention dictates as to how fast a concept turns into physical reality- a physical reality that is tempered as an unbreakable legacy. As our sovereign focus gives us more transformative energy in a minute than a year's worth of linear time. A linear time spent scrolling and acting in urgency. Removing the wait for time to deliver the outcome, as our attention acts as the coolant or the acceleration of time. Whereby identifying the outcome, we have carved the shape of the task. As with attention bending time to fit that shape.

Viewing time as a fluid state- not a linear state. Time through our attention stops being a measurement but a conveyor belt of our motions, inevitably leading to a slip stream state. As our attention has now been compressed into a high density "now" state, where our motion loses all friction. Leading to us not moving, but the legacy being pulled by the vacuum of our focus. Giving way to time becoming synchronized with our natural frequencies. Leading to a perfectly timed harmonic, as time holds the beat. With our motion being the dance. Giving way to casual momentum- we don't move through time anymore. Time is the oil; the lubricant for our motions.

With the cyclical nature of the fluid time of our sovereign legacy. Our motions now swing around to hit our identity, in a sense of structural reinforcement. Our abstract identity becomes removed, with our motions becoming a solid state. With the loop being completed, moving from the stencil that we identified. To our attention, filling the mold through our focus. Controlled by the time we take of setting ourselves in motion. Allowing us to identify the transformation. Instantly recalibrating our identity for the next loop.

With our motion completing each arc, we start layering facts over our intents- building an armor around us. With our motion, as it touches our identity again. The next phase of identification begins for the next loop, where our identity begins anew on a higher baseline. As now, we are no longer trapped in a repeating loop just as within the outrage matrix. We start spiraling, as we are not performing in a closed loop anymore. We are in a perpetual feedback loop.

We can view this feedback loop as a closure to our own sovereign loop. Where now, our motion is routed back as the input of our identities. All the while, creating a self amplifying and self regulating circuit. Where we move away from just spinning in a circle, to evolving as a learning machine. All leading to an identity consistent state, from identity that is shaped from our motions. All the while, being balanced as we compare the state of our motion to the stencil we identified. To stay in focus, to feel our attention is being pulled away. While the feedback loop determines the delay in the time the message of our motions return to our identity. To determine the effectiveness and coherence of the loop.

As the feedback loop comes online, the friction of doing becomes our efficiency in just being. Now, our identity, attention, time, and motion are no longer a sequence- but a resonant field around us. The feedback loops that we have created, have now moved from a loop itself. It has moved into the state of a spiral staircase as the loop becomes more coherent- we begin to move up. With our internal frequencies as our baselines, our intentions and results occupy the same time. As there is no delay between our attention and the motion it creates. Allowing us to break the external noise around us; to become impenetrable to the noise as it simply bounces off us. Leading to us being the project in motion; not just managing the task. Which leads to the temporal stability of our motions.

As now that we have achieved coherence within the loop, we must look at how we keep temporal stability from not becoming eroded. Or corrupted and delayed by our attention flickering. When our attention starts to flicker, time begins to shake causing our motion to weaken from the micro fractures caused by the shaking. In return, weakens our identity reinforcement.

By maintaining our temporal stability through our internal frequencies, we lock ourselves into our natural frequencies. To ensure that our internal frequencies become a metronome allowing the time of the task to become synchronized with the time of the environment. All the while, removing the jitter. Smoothing out the friction between our action and rest, removing the stop-start linear effort from our identities. Allowing for a smooth, constant, silent laminar flow. Bringing us to peak temporal stability, as the loop transcends the beginning, middle, and end. Pushing our sovereign legacy into a state of continuous presence, keeping our motion always happening. Our identity always stays reinforced, giving us instantaneous feedback. Pushing us out of a feedback loop, into an upwards spiral. Further continuing the evolution of our identities.

It does feel like quite the hike through the jungle, as for now. I do believe it is time for a brief interlude, with a moment to reflect upon the dense jungle that we have walked through. There really are no landmarks to keep the bearings straight, walking through such dense foliage. Leaving one to become disoriented, walking around in circles. Now that we have passed through the jungle to sit on its edge. It does feel like the right time to light a campfire and reflect before moving forwards. As it does feel that such a simple concept is hard to take in. So, reflection it is as the sun crests the horizon. Bringing with it the darkness of the night. Leaving nothing to be seen but the orange glow of the flickering flames of the fire. Reaching up into the dusk sky, illuminating the jungle that lies feet behind us.

It is rather relaxing sitting by an open flame with the day turning to night. Further amplifying the glows on the surrounding environment. Like a beacon, lighting the way for rest in their travels. That there are other travelers out in the world as well, all sitting around their own fires watching the flames burn away the woods. For myself, I find it easy to lose myself in the dancing flames, being mesmerized in a trance like state. Watching the flames dance to and fro, ultimately spiraling up into the night sky. Twirling around an unseen force, creating a vortex in its dance. Almost like there are two different flames interacting, pushing upwards on the drafts of the heat. As well as pushing downward from the cool evening air. Slowing the heat while speeding up the heat. Just as our attention accelerates time or decelerates time.

One can almost say the flame we see could represent our creation and alignment- a white flame. Projecting a warmth and radiance of our external awareness, showing the light of identity to the world. As in a visible light of our awareness, allowing the world to see the results of our tasks tied to our natural frequencies. A flame that is our creation and alignment, a frequency that allows us to author our own lives. Acting as an accelerant in our cyclical time. As the flames swirl in their dance upon the night sky, illuminating the area in a warm glow of orange light. Another flame plays its part in the white flames dance. A darker, unseen flame- a black flame that puts downwards pressure on the white flame. Almost like an opposite counteracting the other flame.

A black flame that could be seen as the heat of our identities, as it consumes and transmutes the external world around. Almost like a furnace that burns away the external pulses of the world. As it is a dark flame that represents our sovereign selves that leads to the fire of dissolution. Powering us to say "no." A flame that can be turned into a frequency to incinerate the external pulses of urgency, guilt, and obligations. To be used as an anchor to our internal selves to allow us to nullify the hooks of the matrix. Allowing us to burn away all non-sovereign pulses, transforming the pulse back into neutral energy. All the while, being a dark, silent flame that is contractive- a de-accelerant to the fluid motion of time.

In a sense, many call the white and black flames many things. The yin and yang comes to mind, being a rather abstract example of them. As they do not coincide without each other, as the swirling up the campfire flames show. It is a harmonic dance being played out, for when the dark flame is not swirling with the white flame. The white flame just drifts along the top of the burning logs, barely burning. Just giving us enough life to see. With only the black flame, the power of the flame pushes down upon the burning logs in no direction at all. Ultimately snuffing the burning logs from its cold absolution.

Looking now at the fire burning intently away. It is two different flames at action, creating a loop of heating and cooling- a convection current if you will. Ultimately creating a power of its own, spiraling and rising upwards in the sky. Just as with the feedback loop of our own sovereign loops.

As the morning sun peaks over the horizon, slowly illuminating the field around us. Awakening the birds nestled in the jungle behind us, gleefully chirping away to a new day. With the smoldering ashes of the night's fire gone. I do believe it is time to move on down the path that lies ahead. I must admit, as the great chaos coliseum of the outrage matrix is far in the past. The atmosphere has definitely changed- to a lower frequency. Almost like a hum on the backdrop of the environment around. A frequency of Mother Nature that resonates with our own internal frequencies. Like a soft noise that sits at the edges of our ears, just quietly resonating like a tuning fork throughout our nervous systems.

At some point, I am sure the focal point of the frequency of mother nature will show itself. Just as the focal point of our sovereign loops. Just like the white and black flames of the campfire. We can see that they are two forces working in tandem, just like the cathodes and anodes of a battery. To power us forward or slow us down. Just as our absolute attention on a single point compacts time, while diffusing our attention slows time. Creating a displacement as now the black flame of our sovereign selves that provides the heat and catalyst to lock our attentions into a time flow. Allowing our motion to become self-sustaining with the loop creating itself. A loop that spins faster upon each revolution of our sovereign loop. Building upon itself to step up the staircase to a new platform, where we can stop and view our previous identities.

It is not as much as standing on a platform to view our previous identities, as at the end of each loop our decisions become absolute. Just as with the sovereign legacy of our motions. Locking us in to see that all decisions we make are irreversible. It is the realization of seeing the mutations in our identities as we complete a loop-building upon our old identities to refine them. As the temporal stability speeds up, as now the loop surrounds us. Pushing out from the gravity well of our own internal roots, to engage with the cyclical feedback loop we have now created. Our identities stop being the fixed point; it becomes a vector. As now the fixed point is the gravity we create for ourselves, from being unmoving to the external pulses. Just as with the mountain standing tall against the flowing fog- we become ourselves.

With the increasing speed of our feedback loops, spinning around us. Our motion starts throwing off the traits that we identify as not resonating with our internal frequencies.

To be incinerated by the black flame that says, "no." Where now we are recoding our identity in real time as by the time the loop returns to the start.

We have already upgraded ourselves. Leading to the sovereign singularity that lies at the heart of our gravity. A point where our identities and motions merge, leaving our identities in a fluid and expanding states. As now our sovereign legacy is not something we build; it's the trail we leave behind.

As our feedback loops increases in velocity around us, it hits the boundary layer that we have created to protect our system's coherence. Ensuring that our internal temporal stability is not interfered upon by the attention of the external world. With our feedback loops accelerating, the internal pressure of the loop increases. Where our containment fields turn the energy into our casual power. Creating a mirror finish of our identity evolution. To where a mirror polish of our sovereign legacies reflects back the non-resonant frequencies around us. All the while, keeping our internal frequencies pure, allowing us to transition from a process we manage. To a state that we inhabit. As our frequencies move through layer- internal, natural, baseline, and finally the global field- each one locking us deeper into coherence.

Now we move beyond analyzing the loop, connecting our identity and motion seamlessly. As now our intent and results operate at the same frequency. Shifting our sovereign legacy from linear thinking to multi-dimensional operations. Through providing the power to host our legacy's complexities, while not becoming fatigued. Giving us an invisible resonance, as our feedback loops stay active in the backgrounds of our lives. Allowing our legacies to stay active while we rest. All the while smoothing any friction in our temporal stability. To ensure our identity evolution keeps moving in a silent, unstoppable flow. Leading to the seal of our sovereignty.

Now that we have moved away from seeing our sovereign legacies as a process in motion, it becomes an immutable law in our realities. A seal that we can use in our sovereign loops to become the atmospheric pressure of our existence. As our sovereign loop stops being something we do. As the seal is not a physical object, but a resonant lock, the seal locks our identities into the natural frequency of the earth. Anchoring us to the global field, removing the personal efforts from our legacies and turning it into a natural law. With our black flames branding our loops into a permanent frequency within the system. Allowing our temporal stability and motion to operate at a normal tempo even when our attentions pivot elsewhere. All the while, creating an impermeable boundary, as to broadcast our casual signals out.

Leaving the noise and external pulses locked out. Creating a pure and contained feedback loop within us.

With the final movements of our sovereign loops our casual permanence transitions us as our sovereign ceases to be a project. It becomes fact. Where the inertia of the mass we have created, allowing our motion to move because it is- not because we are doing it. Leaving us to become immune to the external pulses, as our reality has become locked with the earth's baseline frequency. With any external pulses that try and attempt to disrupt our identity and time. Simply flows off us, as we now have temporal armor. As our black flames automatically fills in the micro fractures created by the external pulses, through our feedback loops. Leaving our identity in an automated permanent directive. Giving way to the casual permanence, as after the task is complete. We realize that the change and task has now become irreversible.

Chapter 13: The Quiet Horizon.

It is quite remarkable watching the metamorphosis of the world at this time of year, sitting here on this Sunday of reflection. As the cold icy grips of winter is finally releasing itself from the world around. Not that it wants to as the ground is still covered in the white vastness of snow. Some days it is so blinding as the early spring sun reflects off the ground. Other days, it is still grey. Just as the darker days of the year. However, the change is inevitable as the days of snow falling from the sky. Is now being replaced by the rains falling from the sky. It is rather surreal to see such days; rain pouring from the skies into mountains of snow. I must admit, it does speed up the transition. Soon the snow will be gone, first turning this part of the world into a muddy quagmire before drying in the spring heat. To become spring.

As with this time of year, there are other signs of the approaching change in the year. As off in the distance scampering across the snow, two squirrels run in the distance. Already awakened from their long winter hibernation, chattering away to each other. As they search for their food stashes prepared before the turn of winter. Even the skies have begun to speak as the first of the songbirds returning from their winter flights- singing and calling each other. Dancing from branch to branch, looking for a tidbit of food here and there. All the while, pairs of geese flying low in the air. Looking for a place to land, in the land that is still snow. The geese, I must admit. They are rather comical as they fly by honking away. As if they are honking out, "what in tarnation?" (In reality, it sounds like a four-letter word starting with "F". But I will leave it at that.)

In my own internal world, as I sit back watching the world transform to its own geological clock. I have officially made it past the four-month mark of my digital celibacy. Yesterday, March 20, 2026, was the day. As I reflect on the last months of my life. I can say one thing, nothing bad has happened. I have no regrets, or remorse of leaving the rented wars and outrage matrix. Nor will I ever return to that world as now; I have entrained myself to the silence and stillness. Leaving just a feeling of clarity, as well as the most peculiar side effects- I have noticed that my taste and smell has become very acute.

In all honesty, I speculate that my senses becoming acute is directly tied to leaving the matrix. As the matrix does operate on a low amplitude, high frequency that leads to the panic frequency. As now that the hooks have been truly cut, the vibrations are incompatible with mine. As our identities are not scanning for threats anymore. It is scanning for resonance with the chaos of the outrage matrix far on the horizon. In a place where the noise cannot hijack our nervous systems, not breaking our internal roots. A place where our bodies feel safe; to be able to relax away from the constant high frequency pulses of the matrix. No longer do we need to feel that we are in a constant state of fight or flight- a state where our senses return to us. It is quite the feeling I just admit. But alas, as the days move forward. It is time to prepare for another week of coexisting with those that feel that living in the outrage matrix.

It is always Mondays that are the drag on the internal tempo, as people show up still groggy from the weekends. It is a phenomenon that resonates with many; knowing that it will be another five days of living with the constant external pulses of the world. It is almost like others show up in apprehension of the tasks set forth- just a cloud of doom hanging in the air. A cloud that has no place in a sovereign's world. As for myself, I enjoy the new start to the week. As it is another page in life turned, with just another empty page to write the story of my life on- a full week of life ahead of me. Not written by others, but written by myself. So looking at Mondays, I am always happy. I wake up on my own terms, usually early as to catch the morning sun. To take my time to get myself ready; to march to my own tempo. As I know what the atmosphere of the collective persona will be, when I get to my job.

Instead of being pulled into the herd mentality of the rest, I take my time to offer up small talk. To gauge the attitudes of the others. To engage with them to pull them out of their Monday morning blues- to crack the odd joke. All the while asking how their weekend was, in a bid to lift the vibrational frequencies of the others. Showing by example as the beacon in the room, that being at work is not skulduggery. But a place to create with our time, as well as to have a bit of fun.

As that is what life is about; not to take it so seriously that a person gets worked up in knots from unrealistic expectations. As there are no obligations, nor do we have to feel guilty of not meeting the expectations of what others expect. I must admit, it is certainly an aspect of life as everyone expects their projects done first. As if they are unique to the world, where they can cut the line of others. So as to get them back on their own artificial timelines. Just as the ones that expect things to be completed yesterday; they are always the ones that get told it will be completed in a couple of days. For they have to wait just like everyone else.

It is a concept that many don't hear. To be told they will have to wait, as though they don't understand that things take time. Where no one in this world has a magic wand, to instantaneously make things happen. To accommodate others in their mismanagement of their own time. I am sure it is a concept many have run into before in life- drop what you are doing and do my project now because I told you. Honestly, it is great if you can convince others to react like that. But then again, it is only you and I who hold the sway over our own sovereignty- no one else. At the end of it, that is what we chalked it up to. The mismanagement of their own currency of time, thinking that the world moves around them, or they think they hold control over another. Which we all know is the farthest from the truth.

Don't get me wrong, I am not advocating for throwing all to the wind. To work whenever one wants to, as we do go into a contract to trade our sovereign currency for a way to pay for our comforts of home. It is being realistic with the obligation asked of us. Not demanded of us, as the pendulum can swing in the other direction of people taking advantage of the contract. As people would prefer not to work at all, but to still get paid. Within our collective tribe that we work with. I am sure we all have that type of identity we interact with. I have one as well, the one who believes that they can overrun a job. Yet still believe they have met their obligations in their contract, so they do as little as possible. Ultimately leading to friction amongst others, as that is the reason for deadlines to begin with. To motivate people to finish a task. However, as we all know. A person such as that never changes; they are set in their ways. It is their attitude and their identities. That is how they wish the external world around them to view them. With being a sovereign individual, that is the time to look away and past the person. To view them how they present their identity to the rest of the tribe. If they want to be seen as lazy, so be it. It is certainly not worth the currency of our own time to dwell upon, as we all know. It doesn't change anything; it just leads to friction within our own internal worlds.

It is time to go back to the garden to sit at the table. To have a table view of the worlds around us. Where we can finally step back outside from the outrage matrix, to have a full view of the world. To sit at a place that we can truly articulate from. To see and hear the noises around us from our senses. That becomes heightened from the lack of external pulses around leading to a calm, non-reactive state. Today is another day-Tuesday as the week moves on.

So far, it is just another morning. Sitting around in the silence, watching the world wake up. A place where there is no urgency resonating through my body. Just a calm before the inevitable. It is one of the best routines, as I do not spike my nervous system first thing anymore. Allowing my circadian system time to adapt to the world at its own pace. Not to jump straight into social media, to spike my system with cortisol and dopamine. Just feeling the natural tempo of the morning.

Sitting here, I can feel my temporal and kinetic boundaries come online. Leading to the feeling of having the strength to conquer the day- almost like a systems check. A morning calibration to set the tone of the day.

In the mornings, the long start to the day does bring clarity to the mind. As it removes the temporal urgency of being somewhere on time. Just as the transit from my insulated home to the place of my employment. Leaving at a specific time makes all the difference in the tone that is set for the day. As it is the difference of a commute that is relatively quiet, determined by my own pace. Or to be caught up in the urgencies of others; racing to their own places of work. Where the rules of the roads are largely ignored. Almost like a free for all on the roads, leading to a jittering of my nervous system- minor micro fractures in my own sovereign armor. A jittery feeling that does not last long, as I sit ready for the day to begin. Taking the time for a couple of deep breaths, some morning stretches. All the while ignoring the external pulses around me- relaxing my vagus system. To set my internal frequency into a relaxed state. Readying myself for another day of creation.

Don’t get me wrong, in terms of working with deadlines overhead. Working at our own tempos is not being lazy or not working at all. It is about working at our own sovereign pace to complete tasks- any task in life. Personally, my work tempo is rather high. As more times than not, I am being told to slow down because I am moving too fast. Or with high urgency as some have stated. For myself, it is the tempo that I set at the beginning of the day. As I don’t see myself as a fast worker; I reach and maintain the flow state. Dissolving the linear time around me. Dismissing all deadlines as people can't speed me up when they are telling me to slow down. Which is ironic as I toil away, mostly lost in my own world. Glancing out the window every once in a while, to see others speeding by in their own urgencies in life. Where I always wonder, "what is the hurry? What is the need to race through life from one point to another? To neglect the journey in between?" At the end of it all, it is just the pace of the world around as I turn my focus back to my own motions of creation.

For some reason on this Tuesday, the atmosphere has shifted as the tempo all around has become slower. As if life just wants to work in the present. Not in the linear clock watching way, that entraps many- watching the clock countdown to end the day. More like a stillness in the air, as though the world itself has decided to slow the momentum of time. As today, customers walk through the door in no big rush. Just being there in the moment, trying to explain themselves like they are in slow motion. A day unlike others of urgent requests to get projects done. To drop a project, by breaking the attention on one project. To focus on another. It is quite the dynamic of being fully focused on one project. Giving it all the attention that it needs, to abruptly stop. Taking a minute to recalibrate the mind, to continue on. As when the "rush" project is done, to continue on the first task as if nothing happened.

Urgency; there are different kinds of urgencies that spring up. Not the urgencies of the external pulses of the outrage matrix, that some feel the need to drop what they are doing. To check the pings of their devices as if they are missing something. Leading to the assumption that their contracts are secondary to their digital devices. The urgency of a true emergency, for when someone gets hurt. Most times, it is pushed to the side. Acting as if it was no big deal, to continue on with the day. Other times there is no masking the pain, where the true time of reaction kicks in. Stopping everything to make sure the person is ok, while assessing the situation to get them the aid they need.

It is an urgency that is often overlooked, or that most can't deal with. An urgency that most people freeze in the moment, or others jump forth and react to help calm the situation. Whereas the temporal lag talked in the previous chapters becomes reversed. The people that view the external pulses of the matrix; the ones that view their digital devices as their urgencies. They tend to freeze, as though stuck in time, where the ones that don't react to the constant external pulses. They tend to react in a true urgency, or emergency by calmly taking control of the situation. To be empathetic to the wounded person, all the while taking control of the situation. Situations where the true function of our primitive nervous system kicks in. Our fight or flight responses- the true reason the functions exist within us. To keep ourselves safe and the others safe around us. Not as a function that we let the rented wars control us.

Personally, that is one of the reasons for not being in a sense of urgency and obligations, as in one blink of an eye. With one wrong move, someone's world can irreversibly change forever. It is an urgency I take great care of watching out for; hurting others. For myself, it is my own negligence. Hurting others or not acknowledging that I just hurt another. That breaks one of the fundamental foundations of my own internal roots. However, it is back to work while pondering how many people would act in a true state of urgency? As compared to just reacting to the external pulses around? I know I have had to act in a true state of urgency; as the world slowed to a halt, leading time became endless with no thought but an instinct kicking in. The acts of urgency I had been in to help others; it ranged from minor situations all the way to dire situations. On that, I do not believe it is productive to expand upon the details. Just as with our identities and the tasks we perform, our decisions in life are truly irreversible.

It is strange how the concept of manifestation springs up in life. It is always at the right moment. It might be manifesting, or it could be life in general. Whatever one wants to call it, the irony of life has sprung into this one's world. As observing the urgencies of the prior day. On this Wednesday, my own urgencies have reared its ugly head. Not my own personal urgencies, but the urgency of a regular customer. As today, I am expected to fulfill an unrealistic deadline set out by them. As it was explained to me, they need me for a project that will take two days and two nights to accomplish. I assume that means working 48 hours straight or longer to accomplish a task?

Whether their expectations of myself are actually true or not are two different stories. As some people's perceptions of how long a project takes and my own perception of how long a job takes are two different things. Then there is the duration of the project itself. Will I actually work 48 hours straight with no sleep or rest? That is over and beyond the contract I entered with my place of work. In my past, I have worked numerous shifts of that length. Giving myself to the external urgencies of others, to fulfill their deadlines. Working until exhaustion and beyond, as the tasks needed to be done for the greater good of someone else's timeline. Working to the point that time has no meaning anymore. Leading to watching the geographic time unfold, as day moved to night. All the way back to day then night again.

It was certainly a tough life to get used to; working 24 hours a day 7 days a week. Being married to a phone that could ring at any time. To drop what I am doing in life and rush off in urgency, flying by the seat of my pants on directions hastily scribbled on paper. Not knowing when I would be home again. Training not only my nervous system, but my whole body and mind to withstand grueling work around dangerous equipment. As well as the extremely long hours, in environmental conditions that would drive many away. It certainly nailed the concept that it was not a job; it was an adventure.

The layers of identity that it created in my internal self- the high tempo, high endurance, high focus layers as well as a low complaint identity. Has served me well over the years. Just with the task laid out before me on this day. The project is not much- just time consuming. With delayed being added by the customer themselves, as they work at their own tempos. Creating a new layer of friction, as with the urgency they have created, they have created an artificial temporal lag. Almost like a paradox- get this done quickly, but we will slow you down.

I did take on the contract, why not? I am game, no complaining. Just get it done, hitting the high tempo flow state, as well as vertical time. To not even worry about the artificial clock or deadline. Just focusing my attention on the motion, to complete the task. Not allowing myself to fall victim of the external pulses of the temporal delays- to drift without any hooks to catch me. To be anchored so deep in my internal roots, that no storm can pull them from the ground. To focus and create my time, as I do not have the time to spend. Even with the time, there is no point in clock-watching as others do. As it just added to the micro fractures of the urgency of a deadline. It is to ignore and focus.

All the while allowing me to dispel the urgent deadline that will not have myself working such long hours. As it is about just putting in the effort of productivity. That is all they ask for, as Thursday is another day.

With another day written into my own blank pages. The urgency of the day was not as urgent at all. Perhaps to others, but not this entity. After a day of laughing and engaging in some lighthearted humor with others- a way to break the urgent deadline for not myself. But for others as well. The task turned out not to be a 48-hour endurance run as first described- just another productive day. Working at my own tempo and rhythm, ending it all with a pat on the back. A warm hearted "thank you" for helping out, as well as a welcome back in the morning to tie up loose ends.

I nod to the customer saying, "yes, see you in the morning." I silently exit the building to make my way home, as it is not about recognition. Nor is it about self-validation, it is about completing my day. To return to my own insulated home, with an internal feeling of self worth from another productive day. As I sit here looking upon the world from my insulated home reflecting upon the urgency of the day. I must admit there is still some resonant energy still dissipating. As some days, it takes some time for the high frequency state to leave. Or unwinding as some people say, leading to a night of silence and stillness. Where it is not burning off the excess cortisol or the dopamine spikes, attributed to the external pulses of the outrage matrix. But burning off the excess adrenaline from a high tempo, high intensity day. As the evening draws to an end, it does feel great to turn all the devices off for the evening. Letting the external pulses fade away. Just as the setting sun on the horizon, giving way to the silence of the evening.

I suppose some would call this day "thirsty Thursday." I am not sure of the full meaning of the term; a day to re-hydrate? Or a day to water our internal roots to ensure the healthy growth of our trees, to continue flourishing throughout the week? At this point in the day, I could also speculate that the term's meaning is to have an alcoholic beverage, if one desires to partake in that activity.

As that is how the day feels for me, if I was that type. Right out of the starting gate, the storms blow around. Not of external forces, but of internal forces. An error here, a mistake there. Losing attention of the task at hand, misplacing tools for the job. Or just forgetting- a day of internal distractions not blamed on anyone except myself. It is a day so far that feels as if nothing is going right; as if the forces of the world are against me. Leaving me in a bit of a jittery, agitated state of apologizing for mistakes that should not have happened. Ultimately, pushing myself to stop. To walk away from my tasks at hand. To take a moment to delay time to take a deep breath and dispel the storm that is blowing through the branches of my own tree- slow deep breaths. All the while performing minor stretches to calm my vagus nerve. Realigning myself with my internal frequency, to come to the realization that the world is not out to get me.

It is just the fog that is blowing by, as I will not be shaken and moved. As I am anchored deeply in my own roots. To realize that hard days will come, or days that feel like a fog of confusion sits over me. Knowing that the flames burning inside me will burn away the fog around. Where stepping back and acknowledging that the micro fractures created in my identity and boundaries are solely caused by me and no one else.

So here I sit on one of my breaks of the day. Taking the time to recalibrate myself, calming my own nervous system to not allow the storms of the morning. To hijack the rhythm and tempo of the rest of my day.

It is rather interesting how a couple of hours can change the rhythm of a whole day. With time to sit down and relax; to let the body and systems relax and reset themselves. Allowing one to return to the sovereign loop, to continue on with the day in a relaxed state. Returning to the internal frequency, creating a focused state, where the past internal winds have blown by. Leaving no permanent damage, but perhaps a couple leaves that rattled loose. Sometimes it does not take much for the recalibration to happen- just a moment on a lunch break. To sit in silence, away from the noise. To shift back into the sovereign state. Leaving the morning in the irreversible past, not as events to look back on in guilt. But to add another layer to the spiral of the identity loop.
Where the old adage always rings true, “what doesn’t kill us makes us stronger- or a little wiser.” However one may choose to look at it.

It is not about the external pulses that can hijack us to move us into a high frequency, high panic state. Our internal selves can throw us into that state as well. Leaving only us to bear the storms that may come. Storms that will rattle our leaves and move our branches, ultimately passing by with no damage to our internal roots. It is something, how most times we can see the storm coming on the horizon as we can brace for them. Then other storms sneak up on us like an assassin in the night. To try and knock us out of our sovereign loops.

So, here it would be; the last workday of the week-Friday. As I sit here under the flickering led lights, enjoying my little moment of peace before the others show up. Slowly sipping my morning coffee in contemplation, wondering what the day will bring. It is a toss-up in terms of the urgencies of the day. Some Fridays it is a mad panic to get tasks completed as everyone thinks their priority jobs should take precedence over others. As people want to complete their own tasks for the weekend. An ideal that we call mismanagement of their own time, where most people know they want their tasks completed by the weekend, yet they procrastinate. As most of the customers' urgencies could have been settled at an earlier time in the week. Thus, removing the urgencies all together.

On the other hand, the day could end up being a low tempo uneventful day. Just taking the time to finish up tasks to have my own weekend off. To work methodically through the pile of tasks that sit around. With no rush, no urgencies. Just lost in the flow state that comes from the focus and attention I give my tasks. In these parts, that is what really matters- having the weekend off. Away from the external urgencies that the community brings forth. To have time to relax and concentrate on my own sovereign life. As with my contract at my job. There is no obligation to give more of my sovereign time, by spending my time creating at work.

As the others show up, over the months. The tones of the casual conversations with others have changed. It has been a dynamic I have been observing with others over the previous months. If I were to rewind the clock to 5 months ago at the least. The conversations would be filled with the external pulses of the world; as we were all deeply subscribed to our rented wars. Leading to rather heated debates that would break down into arguments, to the point of yelling matches. Where we would all stand off against each other. As one was always right and the other was always wrong.

As much as I could say that it was just the testosterone flowing freely from people, yet in reality. It was the cortisol and dopamine spikes of the rented wars that created such conflicts. Slowly that all changed with my announcement that I unsubscribed from the rented wars and the outrage matrix- a concept that many to this day, have a hard time understanding. As for some, the digital world is their lives. As it takes priority over every aspect of their lives. It is a phenomenon that I see in numerous workshops all around the community I am in.

People standing around, staring at their phones. Oblivious to the world around them, even during mid shifts when all the others are working away. Creating tripping hazards and impedance as they simply do not move. They will stand in others ways, not moving an inch as their screens are a priority than to this around. Some go to the point that if they are not being actively directed or led around. They default to their digital devices. It is certainly a spectacle to see, as some go to the extent to ignore the customers that walk through the door. It is as if the world around them doesn't exist. But at the end of it all, it is their contracts that they are under. Their reputations, if that is how they want the external world to perceive them. That is on them. But I digress, far from the daily small talk of the weather and how our internal lives are. Some try to bait me in conversations by bringing up polarizing topics that are meant to create friction between people. It is bait that I can see all too well when people start talking. As it always starts with “this person is bad, or this event is dumb”, etc. It is at that moment where my own grey face emerges; to let the high cortisol topics drift around me. To not let my own nervous system become agitated by topics that are not soul shattering events. To just sit and nod my head not in agreement but nodding in listening and understanding the point of view of others- to be empathetic towards their opinions, while being passionately indifferent to the polarized topics. Where my response is just a data counterpoint, void of emotion. Just pure facts of information, leading to the polarized conversations coming to an end.

With the workday half over, it is safe to say that it will be a slow rhythmic day. As the urgency of frantic Friday has not emerged. Just leaving a quiet silence, as I go about my tasks. As not many words have been spoken by others to distract my attention allowing the flow state to take over. Just as with many other external pulses that break the mind’s attention, people speaking can be seen as an external pulse as well. Where many will gather around to discuss how to complete tasks, or how to go about them. Ultimately breaking up the daily rhythm, ending up with more talking than putting the attention into motion. Which can be seen as another micro fracture in the sovereign boundaries or a leak of our energy.

I do believe many have been in the same situation- endless talking about an event or circumstance. With no actual motion to follow through with the task. Where people talk endlessly, spending their time. Taking away from the motion of creating time- to have an effect on the external world. Observing the world, it does seem to be a common phenomenon. From the real world right into the digital world, where people just talk and discuss topics that with a little effort. They could identify the tasks and put into motion a series of actions to create a solution for the task. Instead of just talking, tricking the mind into thinking the task has been accomplished by spending the time talking about it. All the while, nothing gets completed. It is a reason to work in silence; to take the energy of speech. To internalize and channel the energy of talking into my attention. To once again focus on creating my sovereign motion to complete the tasks before me.

Here I sit with another week behind me as it is Saturday. A day that I have no contractual obligations to anything. Just myself. A day I spend doing a weekly report with the others in my tribe- my blood tribe. The only tribe that has any meaning to me, the ones who have always been there for me. No matter how far our paths take us apart. As that is really what a tribe is about; family. Not the collective personas from the identity tribes, nor the tribes of the rented wars that expects us to fight for their causes. But the ones that will always be there for us no matter what decisions we make in life. To be there to support us, or to help us when we realize it is time for a course correction in life.

Saturday, in this one's world, is also a day to get out into the world. To accomplish the weekly routine of buying provisions for the new week that approaches. Leaving my insulated home, to brave the masses of the weekend shopping. To push my way through the others that share the same routine. Dodging people as they go about their own business, almost oblivious to the others around. It certainly is a different experience compared to the external actions of work. Where people crowd out aisles as they gossip with others, blocking the way for others as they move about with their shopping. Or others who are running by their own urgencies, pushing people aside to grab their own provisions. To stand in line impatiently breathing on the neck of the person in front. Thinking that by crowding another's space. It will speed the line up, which ultimately leads to annoyance. Even to the people that take their time, walking at a snail's pace. Walking in just the right fashion to not let others pass them. It is almost like a free for all on our nervous and sensory systems. Leaving our internal sensors on a high state of alert, scanning the people and environment around. As our vagal shields become disrupted by others walking into it. It is an observance I see all the time, a peculiar one at that. Anywhere else, people almost always keep their distance from each other. Yet, when it comes to merchant shops, people tend to pile up on each other. As if they were all magnets.

It is not that I am anti-social, it is just for some reason I like space between myself and others. I am sure many feel the same way. There are odd times I may see others that I am familiar with, to engage in a moment of small talk. Before a simple nod to conclude the conversation, to get on with our days. Which ultimately leads me back to my home with my provisions. To conduct the rest of the day at my own tempo. Which some weekends, I put myself on low battery mode. To do nothing except watch the clouds roll by as the sun's rays dance in and out of the clouds. Dimming and shining creating a dynamic effect against the walls of the room. To lie around in silence and just listen to the ambient noises around. Not feeling obligated to do anything, not feeling guilty for just doing nothing. Just feeling my internal batteries recharging for another week in life.

It is not only about recharging the internal batteries. It is about taking the time to reflect on the chapter of the previous week that was created with time. To let the page turn to the new blank sheet that awaits. As every week and day is truly different in our worlds, although we have the same routines. There is always a mutation to the routines that truly makes every day different. Where we could view that time is a conveyor belt; just repeating over and over again. At a relentless tempo, that makes it feel like time is speeding up as we get older.

On the contrary, time is not as linear as most perceive as our sovereign time shows us that time is fluid. As we can bend and shape time, depending on the gravity of our identity. With time speeding up or slowing down, depending on the state that we chose to live in.

As the day draws on with my low tempo rhythm set, using my time to just be in the presence of the moment- unhurried, relaxed. The contrast does strike me, as the world around me moves in a hustle of urgency. As others take their own sovereign time from their own weekly contracts. To fill their days with as much activity as possible, not taking the time to rest their own nervous systems. To show up on Monday, in the same tired state they had shown up the previous Monday. As for now in my own sovereign life, another week has come and gone. completing yet another spiral to the layers of my own internal identity.

Chapter 14: Integration.

It is interesting how it feels that time flies by in life. Not even a minute ago, the mornings were filled with darkness, to go home in the dark. As if the northern world was living in a perpetual state of night. Now as I wake on this Tuesday morning, the mornings are cast in the soft glow of the sun rising on the horizon. Illuminating the world in hues of pink and orange. Providing contrast against the bleak white scenery that still blankets the landscape. As the day ends, the light of the sun now extends long into the evening. Providing a natural ambiance, illuminating my insulated house as the sun slowly sets on the horizon.

Sometimes it does feel like the change in the seasons does sneak up, as the external world stays in its fast-paced tempo. Always forcing us ahead in the conveyor belt of time, that was artificially created for us. After a while, time does begin to feel disoriented as the artificial linear time and the vertical time of the presence diverge into their own paths. Almost like time has split in two- the external world and the internal world. Where the only true anchor point is just an internal reference in the past. A previous day or event. A memory that anchors us to our internal temporal sovereignty, showing us that time has not sped up. It is slowly marching forwards, where we just need to slow down and stop. To remember.

In the quiet silence, when we turn off the external pulses of the world. To sit and reflect in a moment of clarity that washes over us. The memories that return to our minds. Reflections of our past, odd flickers of the times gone by. Images floating around of the most unexpected moments in our lives. Just random impressions and moments that defined our internal identities. To create who we are today.

In the world that has been created by us. All of us, as in humanity itself. We have created a world that relies on external pulses, to entrain our nervous systems. To elicit a constant reaction from us; to always keep us in a state of high arousal. Always keeping our primitive nervous systems in the constant mode of fight or flight. A world that was not created by any particular group, but as a global collective persona.

Although, there are groups that promote the rented wars of the outrage matrix. Ones that dangle the subscriptions in front of us, like a carrot in front of a rabbit. Ultimately, it is up to us as to whether we decide to enter into such subscriptions- our sovereign decision. Giving us true autonomy over our entire worlds. Be it our internal worlds or our external worlds. To return ourselves back to our internal frequencies, protected by the boundaries that we create around us. From our internal roots, to our insulated houses.

Personally, I don't see myself as anyone special. It is a concept that I am reminded daily of from the external environment around me. As the outrage matrix truly despises sovereign individuality, for it feeds off the subscriptions to the collective persona it creates. To remove the individuality from our internal identities, to have us rely on the external scaffolding that it creates for us. By exploiting our primal vulnerabilities, of the urges to be part of a tribe of others.

That is when the matrix truly hooks us, is it not? In a moment of internal vulnerability of belonging. Reaching out to other like-minded groups to feel accepted as we look for answers to the questions that we cannot answer ourselves. Ultimately imprisoning ourselves within the confines of the chaos Coliseum of the rented wars. The place that expects us to leave our internal roots behind, to become a part of the collective identity of others. Slowly leading us down a path that leads us to start forgetting our internal identities. To a destination that we just forget.

That is true when we inadvertently end up at the gate of the prison. When we forget our internal identities, as we begin to rely on our external identities that are pushed upon us by others. Or worse yet, becoming prisoners in our own internal worlds. From isolating ourselves from the external world, in an attempt to escape it.

That is where we must truly look at the world around us, to understand what the external pulses are and how they affect us. Whether it be through music, the collective persona of the communities we are in. To the rented wars and outrage matrix itself. To be able to view the micro fractures of our boundaries, to fill those micro fractures with the black flame of our discernment. Leading to the ability to say "no." With no feelings of guilt, or obligations. Where the external pulses of urgency are burned off just as with the campfire we sat around. At the edges of the jungles of identity.

As I stated before, I don't see myself as special or unique from others. As we are all the same- our nervous systems all run I. The same primitive way, the external pulses of the world all operate in the same pattern. Even all of the subscriptions to the rented wars are presented to us in the same way. A system that has been created to push us into a sense of urgency, to capture and hijack our nervous systems. To force us into the external tempo in which the world operates. A system designed in such fashion with so many different hooks, it seems impossible to escape.

It does feel unrealistic to try to escape the many hooks of the outrage matrix, as it has infiltrated every aspect of our lives. Where we always feel rushed or pressured into obligations and urgencies. Yet it is about reclaiming absolute control, not over the external environment around us. But the internal environment within us- to reclaim our sovereignty over all aspects of ourselves. To become sovereign in a non-sovereign world.

The mechanics laid out in the previous chapters are not about escapism, or running into the woods to become an isolationist from the world. As we just trade our currencies from one form to another. A state that is unrealistic for many. The mechanics are to show that we can live within a world designed around non sovereignty, all the while being sovereign. To become able to engage rather than being consumed. To march to own internal tempos, as others react in states of urgencies.

It is about coming to the realization that not all urgencies are soul shattering events. Where we do not have to instantly respond to the external pulses- to drop what we are doing to think that we are engaging with the world. But in fact, we become consumed by the world. Where we now have a template to create a temporal lag between the world around us and our own internal sovereignty. As we can now realize that we do have the power to bend time to how we see fit. To speed time up, or slow it down. Depending on what state we are, as with the concept of the flow state. As well as living in the present; the vertical time. Leaving the anxiety of the future, or the guilt of the past. Pushing us past the artificial deadlines, to focus our motions at our own pace. Where, in the frantic moments of the collective persona of others. We can stop to allow our nervous systems to relax. Replacing the primal state of flight or fight, with that of the discernment of the black flames that reside in us.

The mechanics are not only about holding our position in a chaotic world but communicating ourselves with others. Others who may be subscribed to the rented wars, whose only narratives are the ones that their subscriptions tell them to say. Where at any time a conversation can become hijacked by the external pulses and urgencies. Forcing upon the obligation to react. Just as with those that bait us into reactive conversations which always have keywords hidden within their sentences.

Where now, we can identify the words as well as the emotions that can keep us from becoming hooked into someone else's rented wars. As it is not about ignoring another and their opinions, or to dispel their thoughts and beliefs.

It is about being empathetic towards their opinions, as ultimately. We are all humans with one degree of autonomy or another.

By using empathy to realize that we are all humans with our own capacity to form our own sovereign opinions, we have the tools to discern how to respond non reactively to others. Whether it be through the use of the grey face, by not showing reactive emotions to engage others. Or by being indifferent to the reactive nature of our communications with others. To look at the world through a non-reactively lens to communicate back, not allowing ourselves to become entangled in the reactive communications of others- to become empathetic as well as reactively indifferent.

It is not shutting down or blocking others that we do not disagree with or blocking ones that hold opposing views. It is about reclaiming our sovereign rights to have differing views from others, where our internal identities are unique to us and no one else. Where just as much as we are a part of a larger collective community. We are also individuals in our own rights, just as with our jobs and careers. One of the places that forces the reactive states upon us, all the while removing our internal identities to be a part of a tribe. To meet deadlines and such. Where we are expected to live in a state of urgency, absorbing the energy into our internal roots. Poisoning our trees of life. As now, we can once again. Use our grey faces to look at such obligations as the artificial hallucinations that they are. To agree with such deadlines yet still working at our own tempos. Using our focus and attention to dissolve the linear time around us. To fall into the vertical time of the present, allowing us to create our time. Not to spend it.

Mechanics that move into the digital world as well, even into the very fabric of our modern culture. As with the frequency entrainment of the activation and pacification arms of music. Designed, by accident or on purpose. To bypass our senses, to directly control the chemical balances of our bodies. Flooding ourselves with dopamine in a way that sedates our systems to remove our individual sovereignty, to become a part of a parasocial group. Through the use of mathematically generated beats and tempos. All the while emotionally smoothing us to the lyrics they allow us to hear.

Or to the cortisol producing activation arm, of intense energy walls of sounds. To the high-pitched vocals, creating a state of urgency and fight within us. Leading us to believe that we are fighting for a cause. All the while just expending our internal energy on groups that just profit, by creating fractures within our internal boundaries. By exploiting our primal fears of aging, being alone, or by creating artificial tribal friction with others.

Concepts all adapted to our modern-day outrage matrix of social media- a system designed to exploit all fractures as well as creating fractures within our internal boundaries. Through promises of acceptance within other tribes, with rewards of validation and emotional reactivity- all systems that are designed to give us a false sense of certainty in a world that has been created around chaos. All tailored to our own personal needs through the algorithms to match us with an artificial tribe, to create reactivity within us to fight another artificial tribe. Tribes that on the surface, appear different. Yet all use the same mechanics to have us subscribe to them. To fight in the rented wars; as there are no true creators of the rented wars. They are just a perpetually mutating endless loop, changing its skin to match the flavor of the day.

All the while leading to the abandonment of our internal identities. Pushing us into the endless loops of outrage, slowly stripping away our internal sovereignty. Until we become fully immersed and dependent on our subscriptions to the rented wars. Destroying our internal roots, only to leave the external scaffolding around our trees to hold us up.

Until we reach a point where the external noises and pulses become so loud. That they start to cancel themselves out, leading to the deafening sound of silence. Where in a moment of clarity, we can truly step back to see it all for what it is. A system designed to entrap us, not through our consciousness. But entrapping us by hijacking our primal fears, as well as manipulating our nervous systems and our biochemistry. Where we come to a point in life, from our sheer exhaustion, boredom, or numerous other ways. Where we just stop.

We stop in a way that feels like our whole external worlds come grinding to a halt. Where the pulses of the external world do not matter anymore. Stopping to step back and take such a deep breath, that our vagus nerve feels the change. Realizing all of the external threats are not threats at all. But artificial threats that we lead ourselves to believe are real. As there is never any actual threat to our lives or our safety. It is just the external environments around us that mimic the threats that trigger our primal instincts of survival. Allowing us the brief moment to allow ourselves to recalibrate the internal environment of our sovereign worlds. To place us in a relaxed state, to view the world through a different lens- our memories. Leading us to remember parts of our lives when we were sovereign entities upon this planet. To remember, that no matter how small the spark of our internal flames are.

We can always reignite our internal engines, to set in motion our focus and attention. To reclaim and rebuild our sovereign roots.

As now, we not only have the mechanics to see the outrage matrix in action. We have the mechanics and tools to rebuild our sovereign roots. To rebuild our internal identities as well as create internal boundaries; to let our gardens flourish as we are the true curators of our sovereign selves. All the while, realizing that the collective tribes of the world. Their labels, identities and rented wars are all just external forces imposed on us. At the sacrifice of ourselves.

It is sacrifice that the subscriptions to the rented wars of the outrage matrix demands from us. Whether the sacrifices be our true internal identity, to fit in with a community persona. Or it be the sacrifice of ourselves only real currency on this planet; time. Or one of the greatest sacrifices of all. Our true tribes- our own blood tribes. Family. Sacrifices that once gone takes work and effort to bring back to our internal worlds.

One of the cruelest ironies of the tribal collectives of the outrage matrix is; the abandonment of our families. To adopt an artificial tribe as family. Tribes that care not about what happens to us, nor will they remember us when we are gone. They only care about us assimilating ourselves into the collective doctrines, to become amplifiers of the messages they broadcast. To use us as unwitting soldiers in their rented wars. To a point that we have a moment of clarity to see the artificial tribe for what it is. We are cast out as true internal sovereignty as no place amongst such tribes.

Yet, the whole time. Our true tribes always remember. They remember every detail of our lives; how we grew up. Our mistakes, our accomplishments. Our tears and our smiles. They remember the difficult decisions we make when it is time to leave our blood tribes. They remember everything, not as punishment. Not as evidence against us in the future. They remember because it is part of our genealogical history. To pass along the stories of who we are and where we came from. To let us always know that we have a true tribe we are always a part of. Our families; the ones that are most certainly, always sacrificed when subscribing to the artificial tribes of the rented wars.

No matter how far we believe we walk away. Or how deeply we become immersed in the prisons of the outrage matrix. Our families will always be there, waiting for us. It is truly painful to see such a cruel irony fall upon us, I am sure many have witnessed it. Or have lived it firsthand.

Letting our internal sovereignty grow within us. We are always left with the option of humility; realizing that at any given point. We can stop to recalibrate ourselves, to correct our courses with our internal compasses. To return to the open arms of our blood tribes. Just because the motions of our actions are irreversible, it does not mean we have to continue down the paths we walk. We can always switch paths, as the strength to do so always rests within us.

It may sound like a small feat, gaining the strength to relight the sovereign flames within. As what some may perceive as strength, others see as weakness. As unsubscribing from the rented wars to others, it could be seen as a sign of weakness. Or a derelict of duty to the artificial tribes, of met with hostility. Ultimately leading to ostracization from the artificial tribes anyways.

Yet is it a weakness to understand that the external environment affects our nervous systems? Or is it a strength to understand that it is, with the ability to take control of our own nervous systems. To know that we can use our physical bodies and conscience to relax ourselves out of a reactive state? Is it a weakness to change our daily practices to match the natural tempo of the world? All the while removing the external pulse of the world by creating boundaries? Such as creating temporal stability, to slow the reactive nature of the world around us. By simply taking a step back and taking slow deep breaths. To gain control over our internal time in any situation? Or to simply adjust our daily lives to match our circadian rhythms, pulling ourselves off the conveyor belt of time? To realize that we can live in the vertical time of the present moment, all the while knowing that time is bendable and laminar to what we want time to be? Those are the so-called weaknesses that the outrage matrix sees, as we remove the hooks from us to regain our internal sovereignty. The tools are not weaknesses, but they are our strengths as sovereign entities. As the outrage matrix inverted these ideals, to keep us from ever seeing our true potentials. Giving reason to want to leave.

Even with one of the greatest strengths we have; changing our mindsets. To see the external world for what it is. Allowing us to truly focus our attention inwards and back on ourselves. To feel the growth of our sovereign loops start spiraling within us. As once we rekindle our flames, we become sovereign in our motions. Creating the true endless spiral that we are meant to inhabit. Not the endless loops of outrage. But in the endless progression of our internal identities creating layers within us, to the point that we do have our own internal gravities. That always returns us to internal identities that has grown. Not in the sense of returning to a destination but returning to the original place that we have started. With more knowledge, building upon our internal identities to create an everlasting spiral within us.

True strength to push us forward, that ultimately becomes a self-sufficient spiral that relies on no external forces of validation, urgency, or obligations. Just whatever our internal rhythms and tempos dictate. Pushing us not only forward but driving the evolution of our species forward. Away from the primal needs to be a part of a collective tribe other than our true blood tribes. But to allow us the clarity through silence, to evolve where we can stand as sovereign individuals in a sovereign collective. And now, in the silent clarity of remembering, we return home — to our gardens, to our true tribes, and to the sovereignty that was never an ending, but the beginning of our spiral, as we walk forward into a world that no longer owns us.